# ZERO DOWN IN PARADISE

## THE HAWAII VA LOAN PLAYBOOK FOR MILITARY HOMEBUYERS

JAY A MILLER

# COPYRIGHT



**ISBN:** 979-8-9963553-0-3 **(Paperback), ISBN:** 979-8-9963553-1-0 **(eBook), ISBN:** 979-8-9963553-2-7 **(Hardcover)**

First edition, 2026.

Published by: Jay A Miller. Printed in the United States of America.

**Disclaimer:** This book is for informational and educational purposes only. The information contained herein is based on the author's experience as a licensed mortgage professional in Hawaii and is current as of the date of publication. Loan products, VA guidelines, tax laws, and Hawaii state laws are subject to change. The information in this book does not constitute legal, tax, financial, or investment advice. Readers should consult with qualified professionals — including a licensed mortgage loan originator, a tax advisor, an attorney, and a real estate agent — before making any financial or real estate decisions. Tax laws change; the VA funding fee deductibility provisions described in this book are current as of tax year 2026 and may be subject to legislative change. The author and publisher disclaim any liability arising from the use or application of the information in this book.

This book is not affiliated with, endorsed by, or sponsored by the U.S. Department of Veterans Affairs, the U.S. Department of Defense, or any branch of the U.S. military.

NMLS information for the author is available at the Nationwide Multistate Licensing System (NMLS) Consumer Access website: nmlsconsumeraccess.org.

**For bulk orders, speaking engagements, or media inquiries:** realitycents.com | www.jay-miller.com

# DEDICATION

For Michelle —

You're the steady hand on every risk I've ever taken and the truest thing in my life. My best friend, my partner, and the reason this book — and everything behind it — exists at all.

You've made me a better man, a better husband, and a better version of whoever I thought I was before you. You've turned the impossible into our everyday, and you've never once let me settle for less than what I'm capable of.

I love you.

And for every service member, spouse, and military family who has ever wondered, *Can I really make Hawaii home?* — this book is for you.

# FOREWORD

by Marshall C. Mower

As a real estate broker here in Hawaii since 1999, I have had the pleasure of helping more than one hundred military men, women, and families successfully close on their first, second, third, and even multiple VA property purchases. It has truly been my honor to attend several military retirement ceremonies over the years. To every service member and veteran reading this — thank you for your service and your sacrifice.

As a qualified and eligible VA homebuyer, you have an opportunity to purchase one or more homes here in Hawaii with literally no money down. In an easy-to-read and step-by-step format, this book tells you how to do this.

Zero Down In Paradise is a treasure chest of practical and expert guidance for VA-eligible homebuyers purchasing real estate in Hawaii. The author's "Pro Tips" offer additional insight into the homebuying process and equip you with a much clearer understanding of the mission. The detailed information in this book will give you a competitive advantage and make a real difference in how you use your unique VA benefit.

The all-important question to consider is this: do you want to rent, or do you want to own? Run the numbers. You may be pleasantly surprised. Every month you make a rental payment, you're paying off someone else's mortgage. By owning, you pay off your own.

Whether you're a first-time buyer or you've closed multiple VA purchases, Mr. Miller walks you through what to expect, what to watch for, and how to make the most of this powerful benefit in a competitive Hawaii market. Use this book as a reference, revisit the checklists and tips, and share it with anyone in your circle who has earned VA eligibility and is ready to turn that benefit into a place to call home.

Mr. Miller's depth of knowledge and his commitment to serving fellow veterans comes through on every page. His goal is to teach you exactly what he wished somebody had taught him when he was a young U.S. Army officer trying to buy his first condo in Hawaii.

With the release of Zero Down In Paradise, I can say what I've thought for years: Jay Miller wrote the book on VA financing in Hawaii.

— Marshall C. Mower

# INTRODUCTION

## FROM COMBAT BOOTS TO CORAL REEFS

I grew up as a military brat. I had become accustomed to moving every few years and actually enjoyed the lifestyle. My family always made the most of each duty station as we traveled the world twice over. Naturally, when I came of age, I joined the Army — much to my parents' love and support. I very much looked forward to the predictability of moving every few years and having the opportunity to explore as an adult.

I received orders in early 2000 bringing me to Hawaii, and once again I was elated to explore a new area. I distinctly remember one day driving over the Ko'olaus, something I truly enjoyed and would go out of my way to do daily, but this day was different. I'd only been here a few months, but I had this weird feeling deep in the pit of my stomach. It took me some time to realize what I was feeling, and after a lot of self-reflection, I understood what it was — I didn't want to leave. Deciding to finally put down roots began with my VA home-buying process in December of 2000.

If you're reading this book, chances are you're in that same position I was. After all, I was a VA homebuyer before I was a VA loan officer. I have sat exactly where you're sitting — trying to make sense of the benefit, running numbers, feeling both excited and overwhelmed, and wondering if this is even realistic or just a dream.

## THE ORIGIN STORY

I was introduced to a mortgage broker during this process, and we became good friends over several rounds of golf. I didn't know it at the time, but this friendship would change my entire trajectory.

During one of our rounds, he asked me an honest question: "So Jay, what do you want to do after the Army?"

I didn't have an answer. With the Army, I had a reliable, respectable, and steady career path — but I knew I didn't want to leave Hawaii. My assignment was ending in 2003, and I needed a new way forward. He suggested I come work for him part-time as a mortgage broker to see if it was something I'd be interested in.

At first, that sounded ridiculous. I had just bought my first home, and although he guided me every step of the way, how would I be able to do that for someone else? But his invitation felt right. While still serving full-time as the HHC Company Commander for the 516th Signal Brigade at Fort Shafter, I began originating loans part-time with Mortgage Masters Hawaii. I'd take calls after duty hours, meet clients on weekends, and squeeze in appointments between Army responsibilities.

And something unexpected happened: I realized I genuinely loved helping people navigate their home buying process. I loved the problem-solving, the strategy, the opportunity to guide someone through such an important moment in their life and be a part of their journey. I thoroughly enjoyed giving folks all the information they needed to make an educated decision and watching their faces light up when they learned this could be a reality. My first year, I originated over $3 million in loans — a sign I'd found my future.

By the end of 2003, I made the jump. I left active duty and joined Wells Fargo Home Mortgage of Hawaii in January 2004 while in the

Army Reserves. It was the beginning of a career I absolutely loved, and I was optimistic about my future.

However, the Army wasn't done with me just yet. I got the call in June 2007 that I was being deployed to Kabul, Afghanistan. I traveled that year between Kuwait, Afghanistan, and Iraq, and at the end of my time in the desert, I was asked if I would "volunteer" to stay another year. Good ol' 2008 — the year of the financial collapse. I can't say I was sad to miss that one.

When I returned home in 2009, I went straight back to work at Wells Fargo — rebuilding relationships in a recovering financial environment, and beginning the rest of my life with Michelle.

Being away for so long and in a truly harsh environment gave me something that a lot of loan officers lost during the hard times: momentum, clarity, and purpose. I knew exactly what I wanted to do, and that conviction carried me through my rebuild — and it's what still drives me today.

Over the next decade and a half, I built a career helping military families buy homes in Hawaii. I've sat at closing tables with everyone from E-5s buying their first studio to O-6s buying their dream home in Kailua. I've guided dual-military couples through multiple VA loans, helped veterans return to the islands years after their last PCS, and walked nervous first-time buyers through every document, every deadline, and every surprise that Hawaii's market throws at you. This book is my way of giving back to every reader — military personnel, spouses, and families.

## WHY THIS BOOK EXISTS

After 25 years in lending, I've answered the same questions thousands of times. Good questions. Smart questions. "Can I really afford to buy here?" "What does zero down actually mean?" "What about the condos with leasehold or high HOA fees?" "Why does Hawaii real estate feel like its own universe?"

Because of Hawaii's market complexity, I've also seen too many service members make painful mistakes — working with lenders who didn't understand Hawaii's condo requirements, getting bad advice from people who meant well but didn't know the details, losing out on homes they could have afforded. I've seen buyers walk away from deals they should have made because nobody explained how the numbers actually worked. I've seen others rush into purchases without understanding leasehold property, HOA special assessments, or the difference between a single family home and a CPR'd home that requires VA-condo approval.

The information exists — scattered across VA circulars, lender guidelines, Hawaii state statutes, and the VA Lenders Handbook (VA Pamphlet 26-7) that I reference every day. But nobody had pulled it all together in one place, written in plain English, for the specific reader who needs it most: a military homebuyer trying to make sense of Hawaii.

I wrote this book so you don't have to learn those lessons the hard way. My goal is simple: to teach you exactly what I wish I learned as a young Army officer trying to buy my first condo in December 2000.

## WHO THIS BOOK IS FOR

If you just got PCS orders to Hawaii and you're trying to decide whether to buy or rent, this book is for you.

If you're in the National Guard or Reserves, living in Hawaii, and debating whether you're ready to buy a home, this book is for you.

If you served in Hawaii years ago, fell in love with the islands, and imagined coming back someday, this book is for you.

If you and your spouse are both veterans trying to maximize your VA loan benefit, this book is for you.

Whether you're an E-6 buying your first condo or an O-4 looking for a single-family home in Mililani, the fundamentals inside apply to you.

## WHAT THIS BOOK WILL (AND WON'T) DO

Here's what this book will do: walk you step-by-step through the home buying process from a military buyer's perspective, explain your VA loan benefit in plain English, teach you how Hawaii's market works and why it's so different, help you avoid the big mistakes, and give you the knowledge and confidence to work effectively with your lender and real estate agent.

Here's what this book won't do: replace the guidance of a mortgage professional who understands your specific financial situation, provide legal or tax advice, guarantee outcomes, or tell you exactly what to buy.

Think of this book as your pre-flight briefing. By the time you're done reading, you'll know the terrain, understand the mission, and be ready to execute. You'll know what questions to ask, what red flags to watch for, and what advantages you have that most buyers in this market would do anything for. But you'll still want a strong team on the ground — and I'll help you build that team too.

## HOW TO USE THIS BOOK

You can read this book cover to cover — which I recommend for first-time buyers — or jump straight to the chapters most relevant to your situation. Throughout the book, look for four types of callouts that highlight the most important information:

**Jay's Pro Tips** offer quick, actionable advice from 25 years of experience — the things I tell every client sitting across my desk.

**Hawaii Insider** provides local market knowledge that you won't find in any national VA loan guide — the details that only someone who's been lending in Hawaii for decades would know.

**By the Book** gives direct references to the VA Lenders Handbook (VA Pamphlet 26-7) and other regulatory sources, so you can verify anything in this book and do your own research.

**From the Closing Table** shares real-world stories from my practice — anonymized, but based on situations I've seen play out hundreds of times. These stories illustrate the concepts in each chapter and show you what actually happens when the theory meets reality.

Every chapter ends with a summary and action items so you always know your next step.

## A NOTE OF GRATITUDE

Before we dive in, I want to say something I don't take lightly. Thank you for your service.

Your VA loan benefit wasn't given to you — it was earned. Through early mornings, late nights, formations, deployments, separations, sacrifices that most people will never see. My wife Michelle and I are both veterans. We built our life in Hawaii because of our service and the opportunities it created. We bought property here and put down roots in a place that most people only get to visit. And I want you to have the same chance to build something meaningful here too.

Your VA loan benefit is one of the most powerful financial tools you will ever have in your life. In one of the most expensive real estate markets in America, it gives you zero down payment, no mortgage insurance, and competitive rates — advantages that most civilian buyers would do anything for. You already have them.

This book is my way of making sure you know how to use it.

Mahalo, and welcome to paradise.

# 1

# ALOHA AND WELCOME TO PARADISE

Hawaii hits different when you step off the plane — the warm air thick with plumeria, the impossibly green mountains, the reality that you're 2,400 miles from the nearest continent. If you're arriving on military orders, you're not just visiting. You're about to live here, train here, maybe raise a family here. And if you play your cards right, you might just buy a home here.

This chapter is about getting your bearings. Understanding what makes Hawaii unlike any other place you'll be stationed, what it really costs to live here, and why your VA loan benefit is one of the most powerful advantages you can bring to this market.

## THE HAWAII PULL

### Why This Assignment Is Different

Service members arrive at Joint Base Pearl Harbor-Hickam (JBPHH), Schofield Barracks, MCBH Kaneohe Bay, Fort Shafter, Camp Smith, or Tripler AMC and go through a predictable arc: initial excitement; sticker shock when home prices hit around week two; and then around month two or three, a shift. You stop comparing Hawaii to where you came from and start seeing what it actually is — a place where the quality of life is genuinely extraordinary if you understand how to navigate it.

The commute from Ewa Beach isn't bad when driving past Diamond Head with the windows down. Groceries cost more, but Sunday mornings at Kailua farmers' markets and afternoon snorkeling at Shark's Cove change the math. The Hawaii pull isn't just beaches and weather — it's the culture of aloha and ohana, neighbors who know each other, one of America's most diverse and culturally rich environments, the pace, the food, and a lifestyle where surfing before work and year-round outdoor training are just normal. Hawaii doesn't just grow on you. It becomes part of you. That's what happened to me in 2000, and I've watched it happen to thousands of military families since.

## The Military Installations

If you're arriving on orders, you're likely reporting to one of these major installations on Oahu:

**Joint Base Pearl Harbor-Hickam (JBPHH)** — The largest military installation in Hawaii, home to Navy, Air Force, and various joint commands. Located in Honolulu's urban corridor, with easy access to Aiea, Pearl City, Ewa Beach, and Kapolei — some of the most popular military neighborhoods on the island.

**Schofield Barracks** — The Army's primary installation on Oahu, located near Wahiawa in central Oahu. If you're 25th Infantry Division, this is home. Mililani, Wahiawa, and the North Shore are your primary neighborhoods.

**Marine Corps Base Hawaii (MCBH Kaneohe Bay)** — On the windward side of the island. Kailua and Kaneohe are the surrounding communities — windward living offers some of the most beautiful locations on Oahu, with the Ko'olau mountains as your backyard.

**Fort Shafter** — Army installation near downtown Honolulu, home to U.S. Army Pacific (USARPAC). Central location with access to the entire island.

**Camp Smith** — Overlooks Pearl Harbor and is home to U.S. Indo-Pacific Command. A smaller but strategically significant installation.

**Tripler Army Medical Center** — The iconic pink hospital on the hillside above Moanalua. Close to both JBPHH and Fort Shafter.

Where you're stationed impacts where you want to live and what you can afford. Oahu is about 44 miles long and 30 miles wide — nearly everything is within a 30- to 45-minute drive, traffic depending.

## REALITY CHECK: THE COST OF PARADISE

I'm not going to sugarcoat this, Hawaii is expensive. Housing, groceries, gas, utilities, childcare — nearly everything costs more here than on the mainland. When you first start looking at home prices, your jaw will drop. The median single-family home price on Oahu has been above $1 million for several years. Condos are more accessible but even entry-level units can run $400,000 to $600,000 or more.

If you're coming from a duty station in Texas, North Carolina, or Georgia, you're going to experience sticker shock. That's normal. Take a breath.

Here's what most people miss: Hawaii is expensive to visit and to rent in, but surprisingly manageable to own in — especially when you combine two things that military homebuyers uniquely have access to.

### BAH: Your Housing Allowance

BAH — Basic Allowance for Housing — is a tax-free monthly payment designed to offset your housing costs based on your duty station's local market. Because Hawaii's housing costs are among the highest in the nation, BAH rates here are among the highest in the military.

Your BAH amount depends on two factors: your pay grade and whether you have dependents. Service members with dependents receive approximately 22% more BAH than those without — a meaningful difference when you're calculating what you can afford.

Here's what most people don't realize: BAH in Hawaii often covers the monthly mortgage on a condo, and sometimes a single-family home. With a VA loan's zero down payment and no mortgage insurance, your total monthly housing cost can match what you'd pay in rent — but you're building equity instead of lining someone else's pockets.

> **Jay's Pro Tip:** "I can't tell you how many times a service member has told me, 'There's no way I can afford to buy in Hawaii,' and then we run the numbers and they realize their BAH covers the mortgage. Don't assume — do the math."

## COLA: The Other Allowance People Forget

In addition to BAH, service members stationed in Hawaii receive COLA — the Cost of Living Allowance. This is a separate, tax-free payment that helps offset the higher cost of everyday living: groceries, gas, goods, services, dining, and everything else that isn't housing.

Think of it this way: BAH covers your roof. COLA covers everything under it. Together, these two allowances significantly boost a service member's purchasing power in Hawaii. They're the reason military families can live well here — not just survive. If you're doing your budget math and only factoring in BAH, you're selling yourself short.

## Home Prices: The Lay of the Land

Without getting into specific numbers that will be outdated before the ink dries, here's the general landscape on Oahu as of this writing:

**Single-family homes** are the most expensive property type. In popular military-adjacent areas like Ewa Beach, Kapolei, and

Mililani, expect prices generally ranging from the high $800,000s to well over $1.2 million depending on size, condition, and location. Windward side communities like Kaneohe tend to be comparable or higher with Kailua, Urban Honolulu and Hawaii Kai even higher still.

**Condos** are the entry point for most buyers on Oahu, including many military families. You'll find options ranging from the low $300,000s (older buildings, smaller units) up through $600,000–$900,000+ for newer or upgraded units in desirable locations.

**Townhomes** fall somewhere in between, often structured as CPR or condo-classified properties. Prices vary widely based on location and condition.

The key takeaway: don't look at the prices in isolation. Look at them relative to your BAH, your COLA, and the terms of your VA loan. The picture is almost always more affordable than the sticker price suggests.

## How Hawaii Actually Compares — The Numbers Most People Don't Run

Here's the comparison that surprises every service member who does it honestly: when you factor in BAH, COLA, property taxes, and the VA loan's zero-down advantage, Hawaii homeownership often costs less out of pocket than comparable duty stations on the mainland.

Consider a family arriving from Fort Liberty (North Carolina), where they were paying $1,800/month rent and their BAH covered it comfortably. They look at Hawaii, see $600,000 condos, and panic. But their Hawaii BAH is significantly higher. Their COLA adds tax-free income they didn't receive in North Carolina. Their property taxes on a $600,000 Hawaii condo are roughly $1,680/year — compared to $4,800+ on a comparable property in North Carolina. Their VA loan requires zero down, while a conventional buyer in the same market needs $60,000–$120,000 in cash.

When you do the full comparison — total monthly housing cost including Principal and Interest, Taxes, Insurance and Associations

Dues (PITI and HOA), adjusted for the tax-free nature of BAH and COLA, minus the property tax advantage — many service members find their out-of-pocket housing expense in Hawaii is comparable to or only modestly higher than what they were paying at their previous duty station. The sticker shock is real. The actual math often tells a different story.

## VA Loan Limits in Hawaii

Hawaii is designated as a high-cost area by the Federal Housing Finance Agency, which means the VA conforming loan limits here are significantly higher than the national baseline. For most Hawaii counties, the loan limit exceeds $1.2 million for a single-family property.

If you have full VA entitlement — meaning no existing VA loan and no prior default — there is no VA-imposed loan limit at all. You can borrow whatever a lender will approve, with zero down payment.

Let that sink in. In one of the most expensive real estate markets in America, you have access to a financing tool that requires no down payment, no mortgage insurance, and has no arbitrary cap. That's transformational.

We'll cover entitlement details in Chapter 4, but understand this now: your VA loan benefit is one of the most powerful advantages you can bring to Hawaii's market.

> **Hawaii Insider:** Most mainland buyers competing for a $1 million home are putting down 10–20% — that's $100,000 to $200,000 out of pocket. You need $0 down and a strong pre-approval. That's a competitive advantage most people would do anything for — and you already have it.

**From the Closing Table: The E-6 Who Almost Walked Away**

A Navy E-6 arrived at JBPHH with his wife and two kids, took one look at Oahu home prices, and decided buying was out of the question. "No way," he told me. "We'll just rent for three years and go back to the mainland." I asked him to sit down for 20 minutes and let me run the numbers. His BAH with dependents was strong. His debts were low — one car payment. His credit was solid. When I showed him that his monthly mortgage payment on a two-bedroom condo in Ewa Beach would be less than what he was about to sign a lease for, he didn't believe me at first. We closed 35 days later. Three years after that, he PCS'd to Virginia, kept the condo as a rental, and the property had appreciated over $80,000. He called me from Norfolk and said, "I almost walked away from eighty grand because I didn't run the numbers." Don't be that person. Run the numbers.

## THE BOTTOM LINE

Hawaii is expensive. That's real. But "expensive" and "unaffordable" are not the same thing — especially when you have access to the most powerful home loan program in America.

Your BAH is among the highest in the military. Your COLA covers the day-to-day. Your VA loan gives you zero down, no mortgage insurance, and competitive rates in a market where most conventional buyers need six figures just for a down payment. And Hawaii's property taxes — which we'll cover in detail later — are among the lowest in the entire nation.

The math works. Not always, and not for everyone — we'll cover the situations where renting makes more sense in the next chapter — but for most service members and veterans who plan to be in Hawaii for five or more years, homeownership here is not only possible, it's one of the best financial moves you'll ever make.

The key is knowing what you're doing before you start. That's what the rest of this book is for.

## ACTION ITEMS

1. **Look up your BAH.** Go to the DoD BAH calculator at militarypay.defense.gov/calculators/bah/ and enter your

pay grade, duty station ZIP code, and dependency status. Write down that number — it's the starting point for every affordability conversation.

2. **Look up your COLA.** Use the DoD COLA calculator to find your Cost of Living Allowance for Hawaii. Add it to your BAH. That's your total military housing and living allowance picture.
3. **Get a sense of the market.** Spend 30 minutes on Zillow, Realtor.com, or HiCentral MLS browsing Oahu home listings. Don't panic at the prices — just get familiar with what's out there in the areas near your installation. Note the difference between condos, townhomes, and single-family homes.
4. **Start thinking about your timeline.** How long do you expect to be in Hawaii? If it's less than 3 years, the next chapter is especially important. If it's 5 or more years — or if you're planning to stay permanently — start getting excited, because the numbers are about to start working in your favor.
5. **Move on to Chapter 2.** It tackles the biggest decision you'll make before you ever look at a listing: should you buy, or should you rent?

# 2

# THE GREAT DEBATE — BUYING VS. RENTING IN HAWAII

Every service member who lands in Hawaii with a set of PCS orders eventually asks the same question: Should I buy or should I rent? As a mortgage lender, I could simply say "Buy!" without hesitation, but that's not how I operate, and it's not what this chapter is about.

The truth is, buying a home in Hawaii is one of the best financial decisions you can make, if the timing and circumstances are right. And renting can be the smarter move, if the math says so. My job is to give you the information you need to make the right call for your family.

## THE CASE FOR BUYING

### Building Equity Instead of Paying Rent

Every month you pay rent, that money is gone — it pays your landlord's mortgage and funds their retirement. You get a roof, but own nothing.

Every month you pay a mortgage, a portion goes toward equity — real money that belongs to you. In Hawaii, where property values have historically trended upward, that equity can grow faster than in many other markets. Over five or more years, the wealth-building math of ownership is powerful.

## Hawaii's Track Record

Hawaii real estate has been remarkably resilient over the long term. We're an island state with a fixed supply of land, strong demand from both local residents and outside buyers, and a military population that provides a steady foundation of housing demand. There have been flat years and dips — the Great Financial Crisis hit hard — but service members who bought, held, and stayed the course have overwhelmingly come out ahead over 10, 15, and 20-year windows. The ones who struggled tried to time the market or sold too quickly.

## Locking In Your Housing Cost

With a fixed-rate mortgage, your principal and interest payment never changes — month one through month 360. Rents, on the other hand, go up. In Hawaii, rental increases are consistent and sometimes aggressive. What costs $2,500 today could be $3,000 or more in five years. When you own, your housing cost is locked in (property taxes and insurance can adjust, but your mortgage payment stays fixed). Over time, this stability becomes increasingly valuable.

## Tax Benefits of Homeownership

Homeownership comes with real tax advantages. The mortgage interest deduction allows you to deduct interest on your home loan (subject to IRS limits). Property taxes are deductible on your federal return. The VA funding fee you pay at closing is also tax-deductible (Chapter 4 covers this in detail).

Hawaii adds another layer: property tax rates on Oahu are among the lowest in the nation, and the homeowner exemption reduces your assessed value by $120,000 ($160,000 for age 65+). For 100% VA disabled veterans, property taxes drop to just $300 per year. The tax picture for Hawaii homeowners is genuinely favorable.

## The VA Loan Advantage

On the mainland, a conventional buyer needs 5–20% down. In Hawaii, where median home prices exceed $500,000 for condos and $1 million for single-family homes, that's a massive barrier — $50,000, $100,000, $200,000 or more.

With your VA loan, you need $0, with no private mortgage insurance. This single advantage fundamentally changes the affordability picture and makes homeownership accessible in a market where many buyers simply can't compete.

## Keeping Your Property as a Rental

Buy a home, live in it during your assignment, then keep it as a rental when you PCS to your next duty station. Hawaii's rental market is strong — demand is high, vacancy rates are low, and rents are substantial. If you're financing 100% with a VA loan and your condo has HOA dues, rent may not cover your entire mortgage payment, especially in a higher interest rate environment. But depending on rates and the property, rent may cover most of it, letting you supplement a few hundred dollars monthly while tenants build your equity. Meanwhile, the property appreciates, your mortgage gets paid down, and you build wealth after leaving the island.

Chapter 13's "Long Game" section covers managing your VA entitlement when keeping a property and buying again. For now, know that buying in Hawaii isn't just a housing decision — it can be the first step in building an investment strategy.

> **Jay's Pro Tip:** "I've seen this play out hundreds of times. The service members who bought a condo in Ewa Beach or Kapolei, lived in it for their assignment, and then kept it as a rental when they PCS'd —

they are sitting on serious equity today. Some of them own two or three properties now. It starts with that first purchase."

## THE CASE FOR RENTING (YES, SOMETIMES IT'S THE RIGHT CALL)

### The 3-Year Rule

**If you plan to sell within a 3-year assignment, selling costs could offset any appreciation — and may result in a financial loss.**

When you sell a home in Hawaii, transaction costs are significant. Real estate agent commissions typically run 5–6% of the sale price. On a $700,000 condo, that's $35,000–$42,000 right off the top. Add conveyance taxes, escrow fees, title insurance, prorated property taxes, and potential repairs or concessions, and you're looking at $40,000–$50,000 or more in total selling costs.

For the sale to make financial sense, your property must appreciate enough to cover those costs and give you a return on your investment. In a strong appreciation year, that might happen. In a flat or slow market, it almost certainly won't.

You also paid closing costs when you bought the home — the VA funding fee (2.15% on first use, potentially financed into the loan), prepaid taxes, insurance, escrow fees, and other closing costs. Those are sunk costs that eat into your total return as well.

### The Break-Even Math

In Hawaii, you need approximately 4–5 years of ownership for the appreciation and equity paydown to overcome the transaction costs of buying and selling. In some market conditions it's less, in others it's more. If your plan is to buy, live in the home for 2–3 years, and sell before your next PCS, the math is tight at best and underwater at worst. Service members who buy, watch the market stay flat during their assignment, and sell after three years often walk away with less money than if they'd just rented.

## When Renting Makes More Sense

Renting is the smarter play when:

- **Your assignment is 3 years or less and you plan to sell when you leave.** The transaction costs will likely eat your gains.
- **You're unsure about your future plans.** If there's a reasonable chance you'll PCS early or separate from the military, renting gives you flexibility without the financial risk of a premature sale.
- **You want to explore neighborhoods first.** Hawaii has dramatically different neighborhoods, even on a small island. Windward Oahu feels nothing like Ewa Beach, which feels nothing like Hawaii Kai. Renting for your first year lets you learn the island before committing to a location.
- **Your financial situation isn't ready.** If you have significant debt, low credit, or no reserves for closing costs and emergencies, buying before you're ready can create more stress than it solves. Get your financial house in order first (Chapter 3 will help).
- **You don't want to be a landlord.** If the idea of managing a rental property from your next duty station doesn't appeal to you, and selling within 3 years is risky, renting during your Hawaii assignment is the cleaner path.

There's no shame in renting. The real waste is buying a home you can't afford to keep or sell without losing money.

**From the Closing Table: The Dual-Military Couple Who Built a Portfolio**

An Army Captain and her Navy Lieutenant husband arrived at their respective Oahu installations in 2016. They bought a two-bedroom condo in Aiea using her VA entitlement — $420,000, zero down. Three years later, he PCS'd to San Diego while she stayed at Fort Shafter. They kept the Aiea condo as a rental and he used his own VA entitlement to buy a condo in San Diego. By 2023, they had two properties, both appreciating, both generating rental income when not owner-occupied. When they both returned to Hawaii in 2024, the Aiea condo had appreciated to over $560,000. They moved back into it, rented the San Diego property, and started looking at a single-family home for their growing family. Two separate VA eligibilities, used strategically over eight years, built a portfolio most civilian couples couldn't replicate without six figures in down payments.

## THE SWEET SPOT: THE 5+ YEAR PLAN

**Five years.** At five years of ownership, you've typically built enough equity through appreciation and mortgage paydown to comfortably cover selling costs and walk away with real money. At seven years, the numbers improve. At ten, you're looking at potentially life-changing wealth, especially in Hawaii.

But here's the real magic: you don't have to sell at five years. If you bought wisely and the rental market supports it, you can keep your Hawaii home as a rental investment and let it continue building wealth for you while you move on to your next chapter. The 5-year mark is the inflection point where buying almost always beats renting, but the long game — 10, 15, 20 years of ownership — is where the real wealth gets built.

### Short-Term vs. Long-Term: A Simple Comparison

Imagine two service members arriving at JBPHH on the same day. Both are E-7s with dependents. Both have the same BAH. Both are looking at the same $550,000 condo with a $650/month HOA fee.

**Service Member A** rents a comparable unit for $3,500/month. Over 5 years, they pay $210,000 in rent and own nothing.

**Service Member B** buys the condo using a VA loan. At a 5.5%

interest rate, their total monthly cost — mortgage principal and interest, property taxes, homeowner's insurance, and HOA — comes to roughly $4,030. That's higher on paper. But Service Member B deducts the mortgage interest and property taxes on their federal return, reducing their effective monthly cost significantly — potentially bringing it much closer to what Service Member A is paying in rent. After 5 years, Service Member B has paid down approximately $40,000–$50,000 of their mortgage principal. The condo has appreciated. When they sell or choose to rent it out, they have real equity — money that's theirs.

Service Member A has a stack of rent receipts. Service Member B has an asset. That's the difference, and it compounds over time.

## MAKING YOUR DECISION

Ask yourself these questions honestly:

**How long will I be in Hawaii?** If it's less than 3 years and you plan to sell, renting is probably safer. If it's 5+ years, buying deserves serious consideration. If you're staying permanently, buying is almost certainly right.

**Am I willing to keep the property as a rental when I leave?** If yes, even a 3-year assignment makes buying work — you avoid transaction costs, build equity, and generate rental income.

**Is my financial situation ready?** Do you have closing cost reserves? Is your credit reasonable? Is your debt manageable? Chapter 3 covers financial preparation.

**How does my family feel about it?** If your spouse isn't on board or owning would diminish your quality of life, that matters. This is supposed to be paradise.

**What does the math actually say?** Don't guess — run the numbers. I built realitycents.com specifically to provide custom calculation tools for Hawaii, including a rent vs. buy calculator that lets you compare true costs over your expected timeline and a custom military calculator that determines your maximum purchasing power based on your actual pay, BAH, BAS, and COLA data for your specific rank and time in service. Plug in your numbers, factor in a specific property, and see exactly where you stand. The tools are free.

> **Hawaii Insider:** "Here's something I've noticed throughout my career: the service members who regret their housing decision in Hawaii almost always regret NOT buying, not the other way around. The ones who rented for several years and left without building any equity are the ones who PCS back to Hawaii years later saying, 'I wish I'd bought that condo during my last assignment.' Prices don't go backward on this island very often."

## THE BOTTOM LINE

Buying a home in Hawaii can be one of the best financial decisions of your life — but timing matters. If you're here 5+ years or plan to keep the property as a rental, the math almost always works. If you're selling in under 3 years, proceed with caution — transaction costs can eat up gains and result in losses.

You have an advantage most buyers don't. Your VA loan eliminates the biggest barrier — the down payment — and your military allowances give you more purchasing power than you might think.

The question isn't whether you can buy in Hawaii. With a VA loan, you almost certainly can. The question is whether you should — and that depends on your timeline, plans, and financial readiness.

In the next chapter, we'll make sure you're financially ready.

## BUY OR RENT? A 5-MINUTE SELF-ASSESSMENT

Answer honestly. No one's grading you.

**You're probably ready to buy if most of these describe you:**

1. You expect to be in Hawaii for 5+ years — or you're willing to keep the property as a rental when you leave.
2. Your credit score is 620 or above (higher is better, but VA loans work at 620+).

3. You have enough savings to cover closing costs (typically 1.5–2% of the purchase price) and a small emergency reserve.
4. Your monthly debts (car payments, student loans, credit cards) are manageable — you're not maxed out.
5. You and your spouse/partner are aligned on the decision to buy.

**Renting another year is probably the smarter move if most of these describe you:**

1. Your assignment is 3 years or less and you don't want to be a long-distance landlord.
2. Your credit needs work — collections, late payments, or a score below 580.
3. You have no savings beyond your next paycheck and no cushion for closing costs or unexpected repairs.
4. You're carrying heavy debt and your monthly obligations feel tight even before adding a mortgage.
5. You just arrived and haven't figured out which part of the island you want to live on.

If you checked 4 or 5 in the "ready to buy" column, keep reading — Chapters 3 and 4 are your next steps. If the "rent another year" column describes your situation, this book will still serve you well. Read it now, get your financial house in order using the guidance in Chapter 3, and come back to the buy decision in 6–12 months. The benefit doesn't expire, and neither does this book.

## ACTION ITEMS

1. **Determine your timeline.** How long do you expect to be in Hawaii? Be realistic — factor in your assignment length,

any extension possibilities, and whether you plan to stay after military service.

2. **Ask yourself the rental question.** If you buy and then PCS, would you be willing and able to keep the property as a rental? This single question changes the entire buy-vs-rent calculation.
3. **Estimate the transaction costs.** If you were to buy a $600,000 condo today and sell it in 3 years, you'd face approximately $36,000–$42,000 in selling costs alone (commissions, closing costs, conveyance taxes). How much would the property need to appreciate just for you to break even?
4. **Compare monthly costs.** Look up rental prices for the type of home you'd want to buy, then use the calculators at realitycents.com to estimate your VA loan monthly payment for a similar property. How do they compare?
5. **Talk to your spouse or partner.** This decision affects your whole family. Make sure you're aligned before moving forward — and keep reading. Chapters 3 and 4 will give you the financial foundation and VA loan knowledge to make this decision with confidence.

# 3

# THINKING LIKE AN OWNER — THE FINANCIAL MINDSET

If Chapter 2 helped you decide whether buying makes sense, this chapter ensures you're ready to buy. Wanting to buy a home and being financially prepared are two different things — and the gap between them is where bad decisions happen.

I've noticed the smoothest home buying experiences weren't driven by highest incomes or most savings. They belonged to those with their financial house in order before looking at listings — who understood their numbers, avoided common traps, and walked in with confidence.

This chapter gets your financial mindset and reality aligned so that when you're ready to pull the trigger, nothing holds you back.

## YOUR HOME AS A FINANCIAL ASSET

### The Power of Leverage

When you buy a $550,000 condo in Hawaii with a VA loan, you put $0 down. But you now control a $550,000 asset. If that property appreciates 3% in a year, you've gained roughly $16,500 in value — on an investment of nothing down. That's leverage: using someone else's money to control an asset that grows over time.

Compare that to putting $550,000 in a savings account earning 4%. You'd earn $22,000 — but you'd need $550,000 in cash. With your VA loan, you're generating wealth on an asset you own with no money down. No other investment tool available to the average American works like this.

Every month, a portion of your payment reduces your loan balance. After five years, you've built $40,000–$50,000 in equity from principal payments alone — before appreciation enters the picture. After ten years, that number accelerates because more of each payment goes toward principal.

This is how military families build generational wealth: through disciplined homeownership — buying smart, holding long, and letting time and leverage do the heavy lifting.

## The Ownership Mentality

Stop thinking of a home as just a place to live. It is that — and in Hawaii, it's incredible — but it's also a financial asset. Every mortgage payment is forced savings. Every year of ownership is another year of appreciation working in your favor. Every month you don't pay a landlord is money going into your own pocket.

Renters trade money for shelter. Owners trade money for shelter and equity. Over a 20- or 30-year military career, that distinction can mean retiring with a net worth of $50,000 versus $500,000 or more.

Service members who bought early and held on are the ones with multiple properties and real financial security today. It doesn't require a finance degree. It requires the right mindset and willingness to take that first step.

# GETTING YOUR FINANCIAL HOUSE IN ORDER

## Credit: What Lenders Are Looking At

The VA does not set a minimum credit score for VA loans. Per VA Pamphlet 26-7, Chapter 4 (Credit Underwriting), the VA's approach is more holistic than conventional lending. They look at the whole borrower picture — payment history, income stability, overall financial trajectory — not just a single number.

Most lenders have their own minimums, and 620 is common. Some go lower, some require higher. But the point is this: you don't need a 750 credit score to buy a VA home. You need reasonable credit history showing you manage obligations responsibly.

What does "reasonable" look like? Lenders want to see on-time bill payments, credit cards not maxed out, and no recent collections, charge-offs, or bankruptcies. If you have older blemishes but solid recent history, VA underwriting is often more forgiving than conventional lending.

**By the Book:** VA Pamphlet 26-7, Chapter 4 states that the VA evaluates credit history based on the borrower's overall pattern of behavior, not a single credit score cutoff. Lenders look at the whole picture — including explanations for past credit problems and evidence of financial recovery.

## Three Credit Mistakes to Avoid Before You Apply

Throughout my career, I've seen the same credit mistakes torpedo homebuyers repeatedly. Here are the three biggest:

**1. Opening new credit accounts before or during the loan process.** That new truck loan, furniture store credit card, or zero-percent financing deal hits your credit report, increases your debt load, and can change your qualification overnight. The rule is simple: from thinking about buying until closing day, do not open any new credit accounts.

**2. Making late payments.** Even a single 30-day late payment can drop your credit score significantly and raise red flags with underwriters. Set up autopay on everything. Late payments are the easiest problem to prevent and hardest to explain away.

**3. Maxing out your credit cards.** Credit utilization — the percentage of available credit you're using — is one of the biggest factors in your score. If you have a $10,000 limit and carry a $9,500 balance, your utilization is 95% and your score suffers. Keep utilization below 30%. Paying down balances before applying can have immediate impact.

## Building Credit From Scratch

If you're early in your career or lack credit history, building it is straightforward — it just takes consistency. Open one or two credit cards and use them for regular monthly expenses (groceries, gas, phone bills). Pay the balance in full every month before the due date. This establishes on-time payment patterns and keeps utilization low, all while avoiding interest charges.

If you can't qualify for a traditional card, a secured credit card works: deposit $200–$500 as your credit limit. Use it the same way. After 6–12 months, you'll see meaningful improvement and can graduate to an unsecured card.

The bottom line: it's not about having lots of credit. It's about managing what you have responsibly over time.

**Jay's Pro Tip:** "When shopping for a mortgage, multiple credit pulls from mortgage lenders within a 14- to 45-day window count as a single inquiry on your credit report. So shop around with multiple lenders without penalty. What WILL hurt you is having credit pulled by different creditor types — a car dealer, credit card company, and mortgage lender — over a 90-day period. Keep it clean."

## Debt-to-Income Ratio: The Number That Matters Most

Your debt-to-income ratio — DTI — is the single most important number in your mortgage qualification. Take all monthly debt obligations (car payments, student loans, credit card minimums, plus your proposed mortgage including taxes, insurance, and HOA) and divide by gross monthly income.

Hawaii lenders typically work with back-end DTI ratios in the 45–50% range for VA loans. With strong compensating factors — excellent credit, significant reserves, strong residual income — VA Automated Underwriting System (AUS) approvals at higher DTIs are achievable, though most lenders apply their own overlays that may cap DTI below the maximum the VA would allow. Don't assume your file fits the highest tier without running it with a lender who knows Hawaii's market.

The VA also uses residual income — unique to VA lending and equally important as DTI. Residual income measures money left over after paying your mortgage, taxes, insurance, utilities, and all debt payments. The VA sets minimum thresholds by family size and geographic region. Hawaii falls under the West region.

Why does residual income matter? A 55% DTI might look tight, but if residual income shows $2,000 left over monthly, the VA sees a borrower who can comfortably handle the payment. It's a more complete affordability picture than DTI alone, and why VA underwriting often approves borrowers conventional lending would decline.

**By the Book:** VA Pamphlet 26-7, Chapter 4 details residual income requirements by region and family size. For the West region (which includes Hawaii), a family of four needs approximately $1,117 in monthly residual income. Your lender calculates this during prequalification.

## Saving for Closing Costs and Reserves

Zero down payment doesn't mean zero cash. You still need money for closing costs and should have reserves.

In Hawaii, a VA loan's third-party closing costs — lender fees, title insurance, escrow, prepaid property taxes, and homeowner's insurance — typically run 1.5–2% of the purchase price. On a $550,000 condo, that's $8,250–$11,000 in cash to close. This is separate from the VA funding fee (2.15% on first use = $11,825 on a $550,000 purchase), which is usually financed into the loan balance rather than paid out of pocket.

Because most borrowers finance the funding fee, your actual cash-to-close is typically just the third-party costs. Seller concessions can also cover some of these costs — the VA allows the seller to contribute up to 4% of the purchase price toward the buyer's closing costs. Still, plan to have cash available. Target at least 2% of the purchase price in accessible savings so you're not caught short.

Beyond closing costs, keep reserves — money in the bank after closing. The water heater will break. The car needs tires. Having 2–3 months of mortgage payments in reserves gives you a cushion and peace of mind. It also strengthens your loan file — underwriters like seeing you're not spending your last dollar to close.

## The Big-Purchase Freeze

From the moment you start the mortgage process until closing day, do not make any major purchases. No new car. No financed furniture. No new credit cards. No co-signing loans. No large, unexplained deposits.

Any of these can change your debt ratios, trigger underwriter red flags, or require documentation that delays closing. I've seen borrowers lose approval three days before closing because they bought a truck. It's entirely preventable.

To be clear: continue using existing credit cards for normal monthly expenses — that's fine and healthy for your profile. What you cannot do is apply for or open new credit. There's a big difference between swiping the Visa you've had for three years and opening a furniture store zero-percent account.

Keep your financial picture frozen from pre-qualification through closing day. Use existing accounts normally, but open nothing new. Buy the truck after you get your house keys.

**From the Closing Table: The O-3 Who Bought a Truck 5 Days Before Closing**

An Army Captain was three days from closing on a beautiful home in Mililani. Everything was clean — clear to close, docs were being prepared. Then, a credit inquiry alert was triggered. A $60,000 auto loan had appeared on his credit report. He'd walked into a dealership over the weekend and driven off the lot in a brand-new truck. His DTI jumped from 48% to 62%. The underwriter pulled the approval. We had to rework the entire file, request an exception, and the closing was delayed a week — causing him to reschedule the movers and spend $900 on a rate lock extension. He got the house, but had to pay off a large credit card balance and extra closing costs for the rate lock. All because he couldn't wait 72 hours. I tell this story to every buyer who sits in my chair: the truck can wait. The house can't.

## BAH AS A HOMEBUYING SUPERPOWER

### Understanding Your Purchasing Power

BAH — Basic Allowance for Housing — is a tax-free monthly payment based on your pay grade, dependency status, and duty station. In Hawaii, BAH rates are among the highest in the military because housing costs are among the highest in the nation.

What matters here is how BAH translates directly into purchasing power — an advantage civilian homebuyers would love to have.

Here's the math that changes everything: BAH is tax-free. Every dollar goes toward housing cost without federal or state income tax reduction. A civilian earning the same gross income would need significantly more take-home pay to match your available mortgage payment capacity. This tax-free status effectively boosts your purchasing power by 20–30% compared to a civilian at the same income level.

When lenders qualify you, they include BAH as part of gross monthly income — and because it's tax-free, it carries more weight than taxable income. This is why military borrowers in Hawaii often qualify for more than expected.

## BAH vs. Mortgage Payment: Running the Numbers

For many pay grades, BAH in Hawaii covers the mortgage payment on a condo — and in some cases approaches a single-family home payment.

Look up your BAH rate at travel.dod.mil/Allowances/ and use the tools at realitycents.com — including the rent vs. buy calculator for Hawaii — to estimate your monthly payment on properties you're interested in. Compare the numbers. For many service members, the gap is smaller than expected, and for some, BAH exceeds the mortgage payment.

Don't forget COLA. Your Cost of Living Allowance is a separate, tax-free payment covering higher everyday costs in Hawaii — groceries, gas, dining, services. COLA doesn't go toward your mortgage, but frees up base pay for other expenses and savings, meaning more BAH can go toward housing without strain.

## Dual-Military Households

If you and your spouse are both active duty, you have a unique advantage: both receive BAH. Combined Hawaii BAH rates can be substantial — potentially covering a single-family home purchase with room to spare.

Dual-military families can also use both partners' VA loan eligibility strategically. If both have served, your combined benefits create a powerful foundation for Hawaii homeownership. Discussed in more detail in the next chapter.

## THE BOTTOM LINE

Getting your financial house in order before you buy is the single most important step to ensure a smooth, successful experience. It's not glamorous or exciting like browsing listings, but service members who clean up credit, manage debt, understand DTI and residual income, save for closing costs, and avoid the big-purchase trap — those are the ones who close on time, get the best rates, and start homeownership on solid ground.

You've earned an incredible benefit through your service. Make sure you're in the best position to use it.

## ACTION ITEMS

1. **Check your credit.** Pull your free credit report at annualcreditreport.com and review all three bureaus (Equifax, Experian, TransUnion). Look for errors, late payments, collections, or anything amiss. Dispute inaccuracies immediately.
2. **Calculate your DTI.** Add up all monthly debt payments and divide by gross monthly income (including BAH). If you're above 50%, consider which debts to pay down before applying.
3. **Start saving.** Build cash reserves now. Target at least 2–3% of expected purchase price for closing costs, plus 2–3 months of mortgage payments as a post-closing cushion.
4. **Freeze your finances.** If within 6 months of buying, stop major financial moves. No new credit, no large purchases, no co-signing loans and especially no new trucks. Keep everything stable.

5. **Run the numbers.** Look up your BAH at militarypay.defense.gov/calculators/bah/ and COLA at the DoD COLA calculator. Visit realitycents.com and use the rent vs. buy calculator to see how your allowances compare to Hawaii ownership costs. The numbers might surprise you.

# 4

# VA LOAN 101 — YOUR EARNED BENEFIT

You served your country and the nation made a promise: in return for your service, we're going to give you one of the most powerful financial tools available to any homebuyer in America. I believe the VA loan is the single best mortgage product in existence. This chapter explains how it works—what it is, who qualifies, and why it gives you advantages civilian buyers can only dream about.

## WHAT IS A VA LOAN?

The VA home loan program was born in 1944 as part of the Servicemen's Readjustment Act — the "GI Bill." When millions of service members came home from World War II, Congress created a program to help them transition to civilian life and buy homes. Since then, the VA and its private industry partners have helped deliver homeownership to generations of veterans and service members.

Here's the key point: **the VA does not make the loan.** Your mortgage comes from a private lender — a bank, credit union, or mortgage company. The VA guarantees a portion of the loan, reducing the lender's risk enough to offer zero-down-payment financing with competitive rates. If you default, the VA covers a portion of the loss.

> **By the Book:** Per VA Pamphlet 26-7, Chapter 3 (The VA Loan Guaranty), the VA's guaranty typically covers 25% of the loan amount. Why does that number matter? Conventional lenders require 20% down to waive private mortgage insurance — but the VA's 25% guaranty actually exceeds that threshold. Because the VA guarantees that 25%, the lender treats your loan as if you've already made a substantial down payment, even though you haven't put a dime down. That's the engine that makes 100% financing possible.

VA loans consistently have lower default rates than conventional loans, FHA loans, and virtually every other loan type — a reflection of the quality of VA borrowers and the strength of the VA's underwriting standards.

## WHO QUALIFIES? ELIGIBILITY REQUIREMENTS

Not everyone can get a VA loan — that's what makes it special. You have to earn this benefit through your service. Here's who qualifies:

### Active Duty Service Members

If you're currently serving on active duty, you're eligible after 90 consecutive days of active service during wartime, or 181 continuous days during peacetime. The United States has been in a continuous wartime period since September 2001, so the 90-day threshold applies to virtually every service member reading this book.

### Veterans

If you've separated from active duty, the same service-length requirements apply: 90 days during wartime or 181 days during peacetime, with an honorable discharge (or a discharge under conditions other than dishonorable, depending on circumstances).

## National Guard Members

National Guard eligibility has expanded significantly over the years. You're eligible if you have 6 creditable years in the Selected Reserve with continued service or an honorable discharge, or if you've been activated under Title 10 (federal active duty orders) for 90 consecutive days during wartime or 181 days during peacetime. Title 10 activation places Guard members on the same active duty status as their regular Army, Navy, Air Force, or Marine counterparts — the pathway that opened up VA eligibility for thousands of Guard members who deployed after September 11, 2001.

## Reservists

Reservists have the same pathways to eligibility: 6 creditable years in the Selected Reserve with continued service or an honorable discharge, or activation under Title 10 orders for 90 consecutive days during wartime or 181 days during peacetime.

## Surviving Spouses

Un-remarried surviving spouses of veterans who died in service or from service-connected disabilities are eligible, as are spouses of service members who are missing in action or prisoners of war.

## Getting Your Certificate of Eligibility (COE)

Your Certificate of Eligibility proves to your lender that you've earned the VA loan benefit and shows how much entitlement you have available. You can get it online through eBenefits, through your lender (most experienced VA lenders can pull your COE electronically in minutes), or by mail using VA Form 26-1880. Let your lender pull it —

it takes minutes and gives both of you a clear picture of your entitlement right from the start.

## The ETS Date and Retirement: Critical Details for Active Duty Buyers

VA underwriting requires lenders to verify that there's a reasonable assumption your employment and income will continue for at least three years. For most active duty service members, this is straightforward. But there are two situations where this becomes critical.

**Enlisted personnel with less than 12 months on their ETS.** When an enlisted service member has less than 12 months remaining on their ETS date — the Expiration of Term of Service date shown on your LES — the underwriter will require two things: a signed statement from you confirming that you intend to reenlist, and a letter from your commander or personnel office confirming that you are eligible to reenlist. Without these documents, your loan can stall.

For context, an officer's LES shows 888888 as their ETS date, meaning their term of service is indefinite — so the ETS reenlistment requirement doesn't apply to officers. However, there's a separate situation that affects officers and enlisted alike.

**Anyone retiring from military service.** If you're within 12 months of your retirement date, the same income continuity concern applies regardless of rank. Once you've submitted retirement paperwork or have an approved retirement date within 12 months, the underwriter knows your military income has an expiration date. You'll face the same qualification challenge.

Why does this matter? Because you may find yourself in a gray zone — you can't qualify using your current military income, but you're not close enough to your transition date to have a new civilian job lined up.

The good news is that there is a path forward if you're transitioning out. If you've already secured a new job, we can qualify you on that new income as long as three conditions are met: you have a signed offer letter showing your start date and salary, any pre-employment conditions have been satisfied, and your start date is prior to the first payment date of the loan.

**Jay's Pro Tip:** "If you're enlisted, check your LES right now and look at your ETS date. If it's less than 12 months out and you plan to reenlist, start the reenlistment conversation with your chain of command early — before you start the mortgage process. Getting that reenlistment eligibility letter takes time. If you're retiring — whether you're enlisted or an officer — talk to a VA lender early so you can plan your timeline. Start lining up your next career before you start the home buying process. The worst position to be in is wanting to buy but being stuck in that gap where your military income is expiring and your civilian income hasn't started yet."

## ENTITLEMENT: THE KEY TO YOUR VA BUYING POWER

Entitlement is the concept that confuses more VA borrowers than anything else — and it's the concept that, once you understand it, unlocks the full power of your benefit.

### Full Entitlement

If you've never used your VA loan benefit before — or if you've previously used it but fully restored it — you have full entitlement. With full entitlement, there is no VA-imposed loan limit. You can borrow as much as a lender will approve with zero down payment. If you qualify for a $1.2 million home, you can buy a $1.2 million home with nothing down. This is the status of most first-time VA borrowers and is a powerful advantage — especially in a high-cost market like Hawaii.

## Partial (Remaining) Entitlement

If you have an existing VA loan — and yes, you can have more than one VA loan at a time — county loan limits come into play for your remaining entitlement. The county loan limit minus the entitlement you already have in use determines your zero-down buying power on the second loan.

Here are two real-world examples:

**Example 1:** You currently have a VA loan on a property in Texas with $200,000 of entitlement tied up. Hawaii's county loan limit is $1,249,125. Your remaining entitlement supports a zero-down purchase of roughly $1,049,125 in Hawaii. If you want to buy a $1,200,000 home in Honolulu, you'd need to put 25% down on the difference — that's 25% of $150,875, or approximately $37,719.

**Example 2:** You have a VA loan on a condo in Kailua with $400,000 of entitlement in use. Your remaining entitlement supports a zero-down purchase of roughly $849,125 in Honolulu County. If you want to buy a $950,000 home, you'd need 25% of the $100,875 difference — approximately $25,219 as a down payment.

**The critical takeaway: you CAN still purchase above your remaining VA eligibility limit.** You just need a down payment of 25% on the difference. This is a detail that many service members — and many lenders — don't fully understand, and it can be the difference between thinking you can't buy and realizing you absolutely can.

## Restoring Your Entitlement

Previously used entitlement can be restored in three ways. First, you can sell the property and pay off the VA loan in full — this automatically frees up your entitlement. Second, you can have an eligible veteran assume your loan and substitute their entitlement for yours — this restores your entitlement. Third, you can use the one-time restoration: pay the loan off in full, keep the property as a rental, and restore your entitlement for your next purchase. The most common way is by refinancing from your VA loan into a conventional loan —

you pay off the VA loan in the process, which frees up your entitlement, and you keep the property as an investment. That one-time restoration is a powerful tool for building a real estate portfolio.

> **Jay's Pro Tip:** "This is one of the most common questions I get: 'Can I have two VA loans at the same time?' The answer is yes. I work with service members all the time who are renting out a property at a previous duty station with a VA loan on it, and using their remaining entitlement to buy here in Hawaii. It's not a loophole — it's how the program is designed. The key is understanding your remaining entitlement and working with a lender who knows how to calculate it."

## BUYING TOGETHER: MARRIED VETERANS, JOINT VA LOANS, AND VETERAN/NON-VETERAN PURCHASES

One of the most powerful — and most misunderstood — aspects of VA eligibility is how it works when two people are buying together. Whether you're married to a fellow veteran, buying with a veteran buddy, or purchasing with a non-veteran spouse or partner, the rules are different for each scenario.

### Married Veterans — Each Has Their Own Eligibility

This is the scenario with the most upside, and it's one I see regularly with dual-military couples stationed in Hawaii. When both spouses are veterans (or one is active duty and the other is a veteran), each has their own separate VA eligibility. They don't have to use both eligibilities on the same purchase — they can use them independently.

Here's a real-world example: let's say the husband uses his VA eligibility to purchase a home in Virginia before PCS'ing to Hawaii. His wife is also a veteran with her own full entitlement. She can use her eligibility for a 100% VA-financed purchase in Hawaii — zero down, full entitlement, no loan limit. And here's the key: both of their incomes can be used to qualify for both purchases. If necessary, we can use rental income from the Virginia property (with a signed 12-month lease, at 75% of the rental amount) to offset that departing residence payment and qualify for the size of the Hawaii purchase.

This is an enormous advantage for dual-military and dual-veteran couples. Two separate VA eligibilities mean two separate 100% financed properties, and the ability to use combined income across both transactions gives you significantly more buying power.

## Two Unmarried Veterans Buying Together

Two veterans who are not married to each other can also purchase a home together using their VA benefits, but the rules are more restrictive.

When two unmarried veterans buy together, both of their VA eligibilities are used for that single purchase. Unlike married veterans who can keep their eligibilities separate, unmarried co-borrowers share the transaction. Each veteran's entitlement covers their half of the loan based on the county loan limit. For purchases above the county loan limit ($1,249,125 in Hawaii), a 25% down payment would be required on the amount above the limit.

These loans require an extra step: the VA performs a second-level review under Chapter 7 of the VA Lenders Handbook (Loans Requiring Special Underwriting) and must approve the loan directly. This adds processing time. Also, the VA is more conservative on these approvals — expect DTI to be limited to around 45%, which is tighter than the 50–60%+ that can be approved on a standard single-veteran VA purchase. If you're considering it, talk to a VA specialist lender early so you understand exactly how the entitlement and approval process works for your situation.

## Veteran Buying with a Non-Veteran

A veteran can also purchase a home with a non-veteran co-borrower — a non-veteran fiancé, partner, or other individual. This is the most restrictive scenario because the VA's guaranty only covers the veteran's portion of the loan.

Here's how the math works: the VA treats the veteran as responsible for half the loan and the non-veteran as responsible for the other half. The veteran's half is covered by VA entitlement (no down payment required on that portion). The non-veteran's half requires a 25% down payment.

On a $1,000,000 purchase, the veteran's half is $500,000 — covered by VA entitlement with no money down. The non-veteran's half is $500,000, and 25% of that is $125,000 in required down payment. Effectively, you'd need 12.5% down on the total purchase price, up to the county loan limit.

That's still significantly less than the 20% a conventional loan would require to avoid PMI, but it's a far cry from the zero-down advantage of a standard VA purchase. For most buyers in this situation, it's worth running the numbers on both VA and conventional financing to see which makes more financial sense.

**Jay's Pro Tip:** "If you're a dual-military or dual-veteran couple, this is one of the biggest advantages you have — and one that most people completely overlook. Each of you has your own VA eligibility. Use them strategically. One of you buys at your current duty station, the other uses their eligibility for the next PCS. Over a career, this can build a real estate portfolio faster than almost any other strategy available to military families. Come talk to me about how to make this work for your specific situation."

## THE FEATURES THAT MAKE VA LOANS INCREDIBLE

Here are the features that set VA loans apart from every other mortgage product available.

## Zero Down Payment

In Hawaii, where the median condo price is around $550,000, a conventional buyer putting 20% down needs $110,000 in cash. You need zero. That's $110,000 you keep for savings, investing, or other purposes.

## No Private Mortgage Insurance (PMI)

On a conventional loan with less than 20% down, PMI typically costs $100–$300 or more per month. With a VA loan, there is no PMI. The VA's guarantee replaces it entirely.

## Competitive Interest Rates

Because of the government guarantee, VA loans typically carry rates 0.375%–0.50% lower than comparable conventional rates, saving tens of thousands in interest over 30 years.

## Closing Costs in Hawaii

In Hawaii, you can pay all customary closing costs. The VA's "non-allowable fee" restrictions only apply if the lender charges a 1% origination fee. Most Hawaii lenders do not, so you can pay standard closing costs without restriction. One notable exception: Navy Federal Credit Union advertises their VA rate with a 1% origination fee included and only waives this fee with a 0.25% increase in the rate. Always check the fine print when looking at rates online.

## The VA Funding Fee

The VA funding fee helps sustain the program. For first-time use with no down, it's 2.15%; for subsequent use, 3.30%. With 5%–9.99% down it's 1.50%; with 10%+ down, just 1.25%. You can finance the fee into your loan — most borrowers do.

**Who's exempt from the funding fee?** Veterans with at least a 10% VA disability rating, Purple Heart recipients on active duty, and eligible surviving spouses receiving Dependency and Indemnity Compensation (DIC). Note that you don't have to be receiving monthly disability compensation to be exempt — a 10% rating is the threshold, even though monthly compensation typically begins at 30%. If you're exempt, this saves you thousands of dollars. On a $550,000 loan, the first-use funding fee would be nearly $11,825.

**By the Book — New for 2026:** The VA funding fee is now deductible on Schedule A (Form 1040) as upfront mortgage insurance for veterans, service members, and surviving spouses who itemize. The deduction applies whether you paid the fee in cash at closing or financed it into your loan. On a $550,000 first-use purchase, that's an $11,825 deduction. If the fee is financed, consult your tax advisor on whether it's deducted in full in the year of closing or amortized over the life of the loan. This is a meaningful tax benefit that wasn't available to VA borrowers in prior years — take advantage of it. Source: news.va.gov/145096/borrowers-can-deduct-funding-fees/. Confirm current rules with a tax advisor before claiming.

## No Prepayment Penalty

You can pay off your VA loan early with no penalties or fees.

## Assumability

Your VA loan can be assumed by a future buyer at your original rate and terms — a massive advantage in a rising-rate market. We'll dive deep into assumption strategies in Chapter 5.

## Lifetime Benefit

Your VA loan benefit doesn't expire. You can use it again and again throughout your life — buying, selling, refinancing, and buying again. The only limitations are your available entitlement at any given time.

## COMMON VA LOAN MYTHS — BUSTED

I've heard every VA loan myth imaginable during the last two decades. Let me put the biggest ones to rest.

### "VA loans are slow."

Not with the right lender. An experienced VA lender can close in 30 days or less. The VA itself doesn't slow the process — inexperienced lenders do.

### "Sellers don't like VA offers or don't want to pay VA non-allowable fees."

A seller's real concern is whether the deal closes, not where the money comes from. A VA offer backed by a strong pre-approval letter and experienced lender is just as competitive as any other — often more so, because VA borrowers have lower fall-through rates. As long as that lender is not charing a 1% origination fee, the VA borrower pays all customary fees, just like a conventional loan borrower.

### "You can only use it once."

You can use your VA benefit multiple times and have more than one VA loan simultaneously. Your only limit is remaining entitlement. I work with service members who maintain a VA loan on a rental property while using remaining entitlement to buy in Hawaii.

### "VA loans are only for single-family homes."

VA loans can be used for condos in VA-approved projects, single-family homes, and 1–4 unit properties (as long as you live in one of the units). In Hawaii, where condos represent a huge portion of the market, this flexibility is particularly important. Once a condo is VA approved, it stays approved unless something significant happens to jeopardize the safety or soundness of the project. Conventional lenders require a thorough condo review on almost every transaction, leading to much higher rates of fallout.

### "You need perfect credit."

The VA doesn't mandate a minimum credit score. VA underwriting looks at the whole picture — credit history, income stability, residual income, and compensating factors. Most lenders require 620 FICO as their overlay.

> **Jay's Pro Tip:** "If there's one thing I want you to take away from this chapter, it's this: use your benefit. No down payment, no PMI, competitive rates — the VA loan is the most powerful mortgage product available to any homebuyer in America. Don't let myths or misinformation stop you from leveraging it."

## THE BOTTOM LINE

The VA home loan is a wealth-building tool for those who've served. Zero down, no PMI, competitive rates, flexible underwriting, and lifetime reusability make it the most powerful mortgage product in America. You've earned this benefit. Now you understand how it works.

## ACTION ITEMS

1. **Get your COE and know your entitlement.** Request your Certificate of Eligibility through eBenefits (va.gov/eBenefits), or better yet, ask your lender to pull it electronically — it takes minutes. Your COE shows your

entitlement status: full (never used or fully restored) or partial (existing VA loan in use). That status determines your zero-down buying power. If your spouse is also a veteran, pull both COEs.

2. **Check your funding fee status.** Do you have at least a 10% VA disability rating? Are you a Purple Heart recipient on active duty? Are you a surviving spouse receiving Disability Insurance Compensation? If you're exempt from the funding fee, that's thousands of dollars in savings — make sure your lender knows from day one.
3. **Share what you've learned.** Talk to your spouse, your battle buddy, your fellow service members about the VA loan benefit. Too many eligible veterans don't use it because they believe the myths. Be the person who sets the record straight.
4. **Start the conversation with a lender.** You don't need to be ready to buy tomorrow. A good VA lender will sit down with you, pull your COE, review your financials, and give you a clear picture of what you can afford — no obligation, no pressure.

# 5

# VA LOAN TYPES AND STRATEGIES

Your VA benefit isn't a single product—it's a suite of tools. This chapter covers the main VA loan types, when to use each one, and the legal protections every service member should know about.

## THE VA PURCHASE LOAN

This is the primary tool for buying a home. Chapter 4 covers the core features (zero down, no PMI, competitive rates). Here we focus on Hawaii-specific strategy and the strategic advantages of using your full entitlement.

### Hawaii's Loan Limits

Hawaii is designated as a high-cost area by the Federal Housing Finance Agency. For 2026, the FNMA conforming loan limit for Hawaii is $1,249,125 for single-family properties. Alaska, Hawaii, Guam, and the U.S. Virgin Islands receive special statutory provisions reflecting elevated construction and housing costs.

With full entitlement—no existing VA loan and no prior default

—there is no VA-imposed loan limit. You can borrow whatever a lender will approve with zero down. A first-time VA buyer in Hawaii can potentially purchase a home well above $1 million with nothing down, as long as you qualify on income, credit, and residual income.

With partial entitlement, the county loan limit determines your zero-down buying power on the second loan. But you can still buy above your limit with 25% down on the difference.

### When the Purchase Loan Is Your Best Play

For most military homebuyers in Hawaii, the VA purchase loan is the right move. You're using the most powerful feature of your benefit—100% financing—to enter Hawaii's strong real estate market. Whether you're buying a condo in Kapolei, a townhome in Ewa Beach, or a single-family home in Kailua, the purchase loan is your tool. Make sure your lender understands Hawaii's unique processes: escrow-based closings, delayed recording timelines, and condo project approvals (covered in Chapter 7).

## THE VA STREAMLINE REFINANCE (IRRRL)

The IRRRL—Interest Rate Reduction Refinance Loan—is one of the most elegant products in mortgage lending. It's designed to do one thing: lower your interest rate with minimal hassle. If you have an existing VA loan, you can refinance into a lower rate with dramatically reduced paperwork compared to a standard refinance. No appraisal, income verification, or new Certificate of Eligibility is typically required. The lender confirms your existing VA loan status, payment history, and that the new rate improves your situation.

### The Numbers

The funding fee on an IRRRL is just 0.50%—the lowest of any VA loan type. On a $500,000 loan balance, that's $2,500, and it can be financed into the new loan. Compare that to the 2.15% or 3.30%

funding fee on a purchase or cash-out refinance, and you see why the IRRRL is such an efficient tool.

## When the IRRRL Makes Sense

Use the IRRRL when rates drop below your current rate and you want to lower your monthly payment without full-refinance complexity. If rates were at 7% when you bought and they've come down to 5.5%, an IRRRL can save you hundreds of dollars a month on a Hawaii-sized mortgage. It closes quickly with minimal documentation.

> **By the Book:** Per VA Pamphlet 26-7, Chapter 6 (Refinancing Loans), the IRRRL must result in a "net tangible benefit" to the borrower. This means the new loan must lower your interest rate (or refinance from an adjustable rate to a fixed rate), and the borrower must recoup the costs of the refinance within a reasonable period. This requirement exists to protect you from refinancing that doesn't actually help you.

## The Seasoning Requirement

Per 38 U.S.C. § 3709(c) and VA Pamphlet 26-7, Chapter 6, you cannot close on an IRRRL until two conditions are both met: at least 210 days have passed since the first payment due date of your original loan, AND you've made at least 6 consecutive monthly payments. Whichever happens later controls. In practice, this usually means about 7 months from your first payment — but verify the exact date with your lender rather than assuming. If rates drop a month or two after you close on your purchase, be patient. Track the market and be ready once you hit that threshold.

### When a Cash-Out Refi Is Better

If you need to access your home's equity—for renovations, debt consolidation, or other purposes—the IRRRL won't help. It's strictly a rate-and-term refinance. For equity access, use the VA cash-out refinance.

## THE VA CASH-OUT REFINANCE

The cash-out refinance lets you tap into the equity you've built in your home and convert it to cash. This is a powerful tool when used strategically. You refinance your existing mortgage for more than you currently owe—up to 100% of your home's appraised value in many cases. The difference between your old loan balance and the new loan amount comes to you as cash at closing. If your home appraises at $650,000 and you owe $450,000, you could refinance for up to $650,000 and receive roughly $200,000 in cash (minus closing costs and the funding fee) for renovations, debt consolidation, investment, or other purposes.

### The Costs

Funding fees are 2.15% (first use) or 3.30% (subsequent)—same as purchase loans. On a $650,000 refinance, that's roughly $13,975 for first use. Veterans with 10%+ disability are exempt. A mandatory seasoning period (same as described above) and net tangible benefit test apply.

### When It Makes Sense

The cash-out refinance makes sense when you've built significant equity and have a strategic use for that capital. Common scenarios include major home renovations that will increase your property's value, consolidating high-interest debt (credit cards, personal loans) into a single low-rate mortgage payment, or funding a major life expense.

Caution: the cash-out refi increases your loan balance and potentially your monthly payment. Make sure the use of those funds genuinely improves your financial position. Pulling equity to fund lifestyle expenses is generally not a winning strategy.

> **Jay's Pro Tip:** "I see a lot of homeowners who want to do a cash-out refi to consolidate credit card debt. That can be a smart move — you're replacing 20%+ interest rates with a mortgage rate in the 5–6% range. But here's my rule: if you do it, either cut up the credit cards or commit to only spending what you can pay off in full each month. I've watched too many people consolidate their debt into a refi and then run the credit cards right back up. Now they have a bigger mortgage AND the same credit card debt. Don't be that person."

## VA ASSUMABLE LOANS — A STRATEGIC ADVANTAGE

This is where people sit up and pay attention, because assumable loans are among the most powerful—and most misunderstood—VA features. When a buyer assumes your VA loan, they take over your existing mortgage at its current interest rate and terms. If you locked in 3.5% in 2021 and rates are now 6.5%, a buyer can assume your 3.5% loan instead of getting a new mortgage at current rates. This makes your property significantly more attractive than comparable properties with no assumable loan in a high-rate environment.

### Who Can Assume a VA Loan?

Here's the part that surprises most people: **non-veterans can assume VA loans.** The buyer does not need to be a veteran or service member. They do, however, need to qualify under VA credit and underwriting standards—the same standards outlined in Chapter 4.

The VA wants to make sure the person assuming the loan can actually afford the payments.

## The Costs

The costs of a VA loan assumption are relatively low. A 0.5% funding fee applies to the remaining balance—paid out of pocket at closing, not financed. A lender processing fee (capped at $300) also applies. On a $500,000 balance, the funding fee is $2,500. Compare that to the costs of originating a brand-new mortgage, and the assumption is a bargain for the buyer.

## The Timeline

Assumptions take longer than a standard purchase transaction. Per VA Circular 26-24-17, lenders with automatic authority have 45 calendar days to make a decision on an assumption request. In practice, the typical process runs 45–90 days from start to finish. If you're selling and your buyer wants to assume, build this longer timeline into your expectations and your contract.

## The Entitlement Trap

Understand this before letting anyone assume your VA loan. **If a non-veteran assumes your loan, your entitlement remains tied up until that loan is paid off—potentially for years or decades.** You'll have reduced entitlement for your next VA purchase.

**If a veteran assumes and substitutes their entitlement for yours, your entitlement is restored.** This is ideal—you sell, the buyer gets a great rate, and your entitlement is freed.

If planning to use your VA benefit again, think carefully about who assumes and whether your entitlement will be restored. Weigh the sale benefits against the cost of locked-up entitlement if a non-veteran buyer assumes.

## Structuring an Assumption Strategically

There are a few ways to approach this. If you're selling to another veteran who can substitute their entitlement, it's a win-win—negotiate from a position of strength because your assumable rate is a major selling point. If you're selling to a non-veteran, consider whether you'll need your full entitlement for your next purchase. If you have enough remaining entitlement to cover your next buy, a non-veteran assumption may be perfectly fine.

Also keep in mind that the buyer often needs to bring cash to the table to cover the difference between your remaining loan balance and the purchase price. If your loan balance is $450,000 and the home is worth $650,000, the buyer needs to come up with $200,000 —either in cash or through a second loan. This equity gap limits the pool of assumption-eligible buyers in some cases, but it also means that when a buyer can make it work, they're highly motivated.

**From the Closing Table: The Veteran Whose Buyer Wasn't a Veteran**

A retired Navy Chief had a beautiful condo in Aiea with a 3.25% VA loan — locked in during the 2021 rate window. When he decided to move to Virginia, a civilian buyer offered full asking price if they could assume his VA loan. The Chief was thrilled — sold at full price, buyer got a rate a full 3 points below market. Everyone was happy. Until two years later, when the Chief wanted to buy in Virginia using his VA benefit. His entitlement was still tied up in the Aiea condo because the buyer wasn't a veteran and couldn't substitute entitlement. He had reduced entitlement and needed a down payment on his next purchase. If you're selling with an assumable loan, understand the entitlement consequences before you sign. A veteran buyer who can substitute their entitlement restores yours. A non-veteran buyer locks it up until that loan is paid off.

**Hawaii Insider:** "Assumable VA loans are becoming a bigger deal in Hawaii every year. We went through a period of historically low rates in 2020 and 2021, and there are a lot of VA borrowers sitting on loans in the 2.5%–3.5% range. As those homeowners PCS or decide to sell, their assumable loans are going to be incredibly valuable to the next buyer. If you're holding a low-rate VA loan in Hawaii, you have a strategic asset that most sellers don't. Use it as a negotiating tool."

## SERVICEMEMBERS CIVIL RELIEF ACT (SCRA) PROTECTIONS

The SCRA isn't a VA loan type, but it's a critical set of legal protections every Reserve or National Guard service member with a mortgage needs to understand. The protection is not automatic — you must submit a written request plus a copy of your military orders to each creditor to activate it. Don't assume your lender will apply SCRA protections on their own. They won't.

Weekend drills, annual training, initial entry training (basic/AIT) and State-activated Guard duty (unless federalized), does not trigger SCRA protections.

### The 6% Interest Rate Cap

The protection is designed for Guard and Reserve members who had debt obligations and then received Federal activation orders. The SCRA caps interest rates at 6% on debts incurred before active duty began, for the duration of active service. This is a critical distinction: a mortgage you took out while already on active duty orders is generally not eligible for the 6% cap.

For mortgages and other real-property-secured debt, the 6% cap extends 12 months past the end of active duty service under 50 U.S.C. § 3937. For all other debts — credit cards, auto loans, personal loans — the cap ends when active duty ends. The excess interest above 6% is forgiven, not deferred. Your lender must reduce the rate and cannot charge you the difference later.

## Foreclosure Protection

During active duty service and for 12 months after separation, lenders cannot foreclose on your home without a court order. This protection applies to all service members on active duty regardless of when the mortgage was originated — unlike the 6% rate cap, the foreclosure protection isn't limited to pre-service debts. This prevents service members from losing their homes while deployed and unable to manage finances normally.

## Credit Protections

If you exercise your SCRA rights — requesting a rate reduction, for example — lenders cannot report that as negative information on your credit report. Exercising a legal protection should never hurt your credit, and the SCRA ensures it doesn't.

## How to Activate SCRA Protections

Submit a written request to each creditor or loan servicer, along with a copy of your military orders, as soon as you receive those orders. Keep copies of everything you send. The protections take effect from the date of your activation, but the creditor needs documentation before they can act. Don't wait until you're in-country to start this process.

> **By the Book:** The SCRA (50 U.S.C. § 3937) is one of the most important and most misunderstood protections available to service members. The key qualifier that trips people up: the 6% rate cap applies ONLY to debts incurred before activated service began. A mortgage you took out after entering active duty service does not qualify for the rate cap. However, the foreclosure protection applies to all National Guard and Reserve members who are activated on Federal orders (Title X) regardless of when the mortgage originated. Know the difference, it matters.

## VA ENERGY EFFICIENT MORTGAGE (EEM)

One lesser-known tool worth mentioning: the VA Energy Efficient Mortgage allows you to add up to $6,000 to your VA loan amount for energy-efficiency improvements to the home you're purchasing or refinancing. This can cover upgrades like solar water heaters, insulation, double-pane windows, energy-efficient HVAC systems, or weatherization improvements.

In Hawaii, where older condos and homes often have single-pane windows, no central AC, and aging water heaters, the EEM can be particularly useful. The improvements don't require an appraisal increase — the additional amount is added based on the expected energy savings. The $6,000 limit applies to improvements that the lender determines will be cost-effective based on energy savings over the useful life of the improvement.

If you're buying a home that needs energy upgrades, ask your lender about the EEM option before closing. It's a small addition to your loan that can make a meaningful difference in your monthly utility costs and comfort — especially in a climate where cooling and water heating are significant expenses.

## THE BOTTOM LINE

Your VA benefit is more than a single loan product—it's a toolkit. The purchase loan gets you into your home. The IRRRL saves you money when rates drop. The cash-out refinance lets you tap equity when you need it. Assumable loans give you a strategic advantage when you sell. And the SCRA protects you when duty calls.

The key is understanding which tool to use and when. A good VA lender will help you think through these strategies based on your specific situation—where you are in your career, how long you plan to stay, what your financial goals look like, and how your entitlement picture shapes your options.

In the next chapter, we'll talk about how to get pre-approved—the step that turns you from a browser into a serious buyer.

## ACTION ITEMS

1. **Know your current loan situation.** If you already own a home with a VA loan, understand your loan balance, interest rate, and how much entitlement is in use. This information shapes every strategy in this chapter.
2. **Monitor interest rates.** If you have an existing VA loan, keep an eye on rates. When they drop meaningfully below your current rate, the IRRRL is a quick and low-cost way to save money every month. Your lender can help you determine when the math makes sense.
3. **Understand your assumption value.** If you locked in a rate below 4% during the 2020–2021 window, your loan is a strategic asset. Before you sell, talk to your lender about how to market your assumable rate and how it affects your entitlement.
4. **Know your SCRA rights.** If you're Guard or Reserve and could be activated, understand that SCRA exists and how to invoke it. Keep your military orders accessible, and know that you need to submit a written request to your lender to activate the protections.
5. **Think long-term.** Every VA loan decision you make today affects your options tomorrow. Buying, refinancing, and selling all impact your entitlement. Work with a lender who can map out a multi-year strategy, not just close the next transaction.

6

# GETTING PRE-APPROVED — YOUR COMPETITIVE EDGE

A service member arrives in Hawaii, falls in love with a condo during their first weekend of house hunting, and scrambles to put an offer together — only to realize they haven't been pre-approved. They call a lender in a panic, the seller accepts a competing offer from a buyer who was ready to go, and they spend the next month kicking themselves. Don't be that person. In Hawaii's competitive real estate market, pre-approval isn't a formality — it's your competitive edge. It's the difference between being a serious buyer and being a browser. And the best part? It costs you nothing.

## PRE-QUALIFICATION VS. PRE-APPROVAL — KNOW THE DIFFERENCE

These two terms get used interchangeably, but they are not the same thing, and understanding the difference matters.

**Pre-qualification** is an estimate. You tell a lender your income, debts, and credit situation verbally or through a quick online form, and they give you a rough idea of what you might qualify for. No documents are verified. No credit is pulled. It's a conversation, not a commitment — and sellers know it.

**Pre-approval** is verified. A lender pulls your credit, reviews your income documents, verifies your assets, pulls your Certificate of Eligibility, and runs the numbers for real. When they issue a pre-approval letter, they've actually looked under the hood and are confident you can close. That letter carries weight.

In Hawaii, where multiple offers on desirable properties are common, a strong pre-approval letter from a reputable, VA-experienced Hawaii lender signals that this buyer is real, this deal will close, and they won't waste the seller's time.

> **Jay's Pro Tip:** "I tell every buyer the same thing: get pre-approved before you start looking at properties. Not after you find one you like. Before. When you walk into an open house or your agent sends you a listing, you should already know exactly what you can afford, what your monthly payment will look like, and that your financing is solid. That confidence changes everything — how you shop, how you negotiate, and how sellers respond to your offer."

## THE PRE-APPROVAL PROCESS STEP BY STEP

### Step 1: Choose Your Lender

This is arguably the most important decision in the entire home buying process. The lender you choose determines the quality of your pre-approval, the speed of your transaction, and how smoothly — or painfully — the whole experience goes.

For VA loans in Hawaii, you want a lender who checks three boxes. First, they need to be experienced with VA loans — someone who lives and breathes VA lending and understands the nuances of entitlement, residual income, and VA appraisal requirements. Second, they need to know Hawaii — not all lenders understand the escrow-based closing system, the delayed recording timeline, the distinction between fee simple and leasehold, or how condo project approvals work on the islands. Third, they need to be accessible. Hawaii's market moves fast, and you need a lender who picks up the phone, responds quickly, and communicates proactively with your real estate agent.

We'll go deeper on how to evaluate and choose the right lender in Chapter 7. For now, just know that this decision matters more than the small rate difference you might find shopping online.

## Step 2: Gather Your Documents

The documentation for a VA pre-approval is straightforward. Here's what you'll need:

**Pay stubs or LES (Leave and Earnings Statement)** — Your most recent 30 days. If you're active duty, your LES contains everything: base pay, BAH, BAS, special pays, deductions, and ETS date. Pull it from myPay (mypay.dfas.mil).

**W-2s** — The last 2 years. These verify your income history and confirm consistency.

**Bank statements** — The most recent 2 months for all accounts. The lender needs to verify you have funds for closing costs and reserves. If you have large deposits during that window that aren't from your regular paycheck, the underwriter will ask you to explain and document where the money came from. Gift funds, tax refunds, and bonuses are all fine — but they need documentation. Avoid random deposits you can't explain.

**DD-214** — If you're a veteran who has separated. Your lender can usually pull your COE electronically without it, but have it accessible.

**Statement of Service** — A letter from your personnel office confirming active duty status, entry date, and separation date. Not typically needed for pre-approval, but critical in two situations: first, if you've recently PCS'd to Hawaii and your Hawaii BAH and COLA don't yet appear on your LES, the Statement of Service confirms those allowances for qualification. Second, if you have PCS orders to Hawaii but haven't arrived yet, your lender can pre-approve you in advance. You can close up to 30 days before arrival, skipping temporary housing scrambles. Your lender will need your PCS orders and a Statement of Service from your gaining Hawaii personnel office.

**Hawaii Insider:** "If you're PCS'ing to Hawaii, you'll receive 30 days of Temporary Living Allowance (TLA) to help offset temporary housing — hotels, military lodging, or other short-term arrangements. With a signed purchase agreement, you can typically extend TLA for another 30 days, giving you up to 60 days total. This is designed to give you breathing room. Use it wisely — and ideally, start working with your lender before you arrive so you can hit the ground running."

**Tax returns** — Only required if a buyer is self-employed or has rental property income used for qualifying. If you're a salaried W-2 employee with no rental income, you typically don't need tax returns. This simplifies the process considerably for most active duty service members.

## Step 3: The Credit Pull

Your lender pulls your credit from all three bureaus — Equifax, Experian, and TransUnion. The VA has no minimum credit score, but most lenders require 620 FICO as baseline.

Some lenders now offer a soft pull initially to pre-approve you and discuss options without triggering a hard inquiry. The hard pull is then done when you've found a suitable property and have a signed contract. This can be a nice option if you're in early exploration stages.

Don't be afraid to shop lenders and have your credit pulled by more than one. Multiple mortgage inquiries within a 14–45 day window count as a single inquiry on your credit report. The scoring models are specifically designed to allow rate shopping without penalizing you. What will hurt your score is having credit pulled by different creditor types — an auto dealer, credit card company, and mortgage lender — spread over 90 days. So shop mortgage rates freely, but keep other credit activity frozen.

## Step 4: Income Qualification

This is where the lender runs the real numbers. Per VA Pamphlet 26-7, Chapter 4, here's how lenders calculate qualifying income:

**W-2 salary and wages** are straightforward — your base pay, verified by LES and W-2s.

**BAH and other military allowances** count as fully qualifying income. Because BAH is tax-free, it actually carries more weight in the affordability calculation than the same dollar amount of taxable income. This is one of the biggest advantages military buyers have.

**Self-employment income** requires a 2-year history, typically averaged over two years, with tax returns. Lenders use your net income — gross revenue minus business expenses. If you've been aggressively writing off expenses to minimize taxes, that strategy may have reduced your qualifying income on paper. It's a real trade-off: the more you write off, the less income the lender sees at qualification time. If self-employment is your primary income, keep this in mind well before you apply.

**Rental income** — If you're keeping a current property and renting it out, documented rental income can offset that property's mortgage payment.

> **By the Book:** Per VA underwriting guidelines, 75% of the gross rental income from your departing residence can be used to offset that property's mortgage payment — even if you have no prior rental management experience. You'll need a signed 12-month lease to document the income. This is a game-changer for service members keeping their current home as a rental while buying in Hawaii. Without this offset, both payments count fully against DTI. With it, only the gap counts. Talk to your lender early.

**Part-time and seasonal income** must demonstrate a 2-year history and likelihood of continuance.

### Step 5: DTI and Residual Income Analysis

Your lender calculates your back-end DTI — all monthly debt (including your mortgage payment, property taxes, insurance, and HOA) divided by gross monthly income. In Hawaii, VA borrowers are typically approved with DTI ratios of 45–50%, and with compensating factors, approvals at 60% or higher are possible.

Compensating factors include excellent credit (700+), sufficient funds for closing plus retirement savings, minimal debt growth, stable employment history, military career stability, and strong residual income exceeding VA minimums by 20% or more.

Your lender will also calculate your residual income to ensure you meet the VA's minimum for the West region (which includes Hawaii) based on family size and loan amount. This dual analysis — DTI plus residual income — is what makes VA underwriting more nuanced and often more borrower-friendly than conventional lending.

### Step 6: Certificate of Eligibility

If you haven't obtained your COE, your lender will pull it electronically through the VA's WebLGY system. Most experienced VA lenders can do this instantly. The COE confirms your eligibility and shows your available entitlement, which determines your zero-down buying power.

## HOW MUCH HOME CAN YOU AFFORD?

There's an important distinction between what you qualify for and what you should spend. Just because a lender approves you for $750,000 doesn't mean you should buy a $750,000 home. The lender's job is to determine maximum borrowing based on income and VA guidelines. Your job is to determine what fits comfortably in your life.

When evaluating affordability, look at the full picture — not just the mortgage payment. Your total monthly housing cost includes

PITI (principal, interest, taxes, and insurance) plus HOA dues if applicable, plus a maintenance reserve for repairs and upkeep.

Hawaii is expensive beyond housing. Groceries, gas, and dining cost more. If you spend every dollar of your BAH on your mortgage and have nothing left over, you're going to be miserable — and Hawaii is too beautiful a place for that. Budget for the life you want to live here, not just the roof over your head.

> **Hawaii Insider:** "There's a term I use with clients: 'house poor in paradise.' It means you bought the nicest place you could qualify for, but now you can't afford to do anything. You're living in a beautiful condo with an ocean view, eating ramen every night because there's nothing left in the budget. Don't do that. Buy comfortably within your means and enjoy the life that comes with living in Hawaii."

## STRENGTHENING YOUR OFFER BEFORE YOU START LOOKING

### Rate Locks and Timing

Interest rates fluctuate daily. When you find a property and go under contract, your lender can lock your interest rate — guaranteeing that rate for 30–60 days while you close. Understanding rate lock timing is important because Hawaii's closing can take longer than the mainland due to delayed recording and the escrow-based system. Make sure your lock period is long enough to cover the full transaction timeline.

Some lenders also offer extended rate locks or float-down options, which let you lock a rate but take advantage of lower rates if the market improves. Ask your lender about these options — they can be valuable in a volatile rate environment.

## Keep Your Pre-Approval Current — and Property-Specific

A full pre-approval is typically valid for about 4 months. But there's a distinction that matters in Hawaii's competitive market: the difference between a general pre-approval and a property-specific pre-approval.

A general pre-approval says "this buyer can afford up to $X." It's useful for shopping, but it doesn't tell the seller much about your ability to close on their property. A property-specific pre-approval is tailored to the exact home you're making an offer on — matching the offer price, the down payment (if any), and confirming that the lender has reviewed the property type (condo, single-family, CPR) and is confident the deal will close.

This distinction is especially important in Hawaii because of condo project approval requirements. A generic pre-approval letter doesn't tell the seller whether the lender has verified that the condo project is VA-approved — or whether they can get it approved in time. A property-specific letter from a lender who knows the project status is a much stronger signal. Most experienced Hawaii VA lenders issue pre-approval letters at offer time, tailored to the specific property. Ask your lender if this is their practice — it should be.

## The Lender-Agent-Buyer Triangle

In Hawaii, communication between your lender, your real estate agent, and you is essential. Hawaii's unique closing timelines — including the escrow-based system and the delayed funding and recording process (typically 2 business days after loan funding) — mean all three parties need to stay in sync. A missed communication can delay your closing by days, creating issues with your rate lock or moving timeline.

The best transactions are the ones where lender and agent communicate directly, keeping the buyer informed and staying ahead of problems. Choose a lender and agent who work well together and know how to navigate Hawaii's system. It makes all the difference.

## A NOTE FOR SPOUSES AND PARTNERS

This book is written primarily to the service member, but home buying is a team decision — and the spouse or partner's role is critical. If you're the non-buying spouse reading along, here's what you need to know.

**You're part of the qualification.** If you're on the loan, your income, credit, and debts all factor in. If your credit needs work or you're carrying significant debt, it may actually make sense for the service member to apply solo (using only their income and credit). You can still both be on the title of the property together even if you are not on the loan. Discuss it openly with your lender so they can advise if there are any steps that can be taken to strengthen your credit profile before finding a home to purchase.

**If you're both veterans, you have a strategic advantage.** Each of you has separate VA entitlement that can be used independently. One of you buys at this duty station, the other saves their entitlement for the next one. Over a career, this builds a portfolio. Chapter 4 covers this in detail.

**Your questions matter.** Ask the lender anything. How does this affect our DTI? What happens if we PCS in three years? What if one of us separates from the military? A good lender will welcome these questions, not brush them off.

**The VA loan affects you legally.** If you're on the loan, you're equally responsible for the debt. If you're not on the loan but you're married, Hawaii is not a community property state — but the property still affects your family's financial picture. Understand what you're signing and what it means for your family's future.

**Support the financial freeze.** From pre-qualification through closing, no new credit, no big purchases, no surprises. The service member needs your partnership on this — one unexpected credit card application or furniture loan can derail the closing. Buy the new couch after you get the keys.

## THE BOTTOM LINE

Getting pre-approved is the single most important step before house hunting. It tells you exactly what you can afford, it makes your offers competitive, and it gives you confidence to move quickly when you find the right property. In Hawaii's market, where desirable properties attract multiple offers and timing matters, the buyer who shows up pre-approved and ready to go has a significant advantage.

The process is straightforward, it costs nothing, and any experienced VA lender can walk you through it in a single conversation. Don't wait until you find the perfect property. Start now.

## ACTION ITEMS

1. **Contact a VA-experienced Hawaii lender — even before you arrive.** If you have PCS orders to Hawaii, don't wait until you're on the ground. A good lender can pre-approve you from your current duty station and you can close up to 30 days before arrival. The earlier you start the relationship, the better prepared you'll be.
2. **Gather your documents.** Pull together your LES or pay stubs (30 days), W-2s (2 years), and bank statements (2 months). If you're PCS'ing, have a copy of your orders ready. Your lender can usually pull your COE electronically.
3. **Pull your credit.** Check your free credit report at annualcreditreport.com before your lender pulls it. Review for errors, collections, or surprises. Ask your lender if they offer a soft pull to get started without a hard inquiry.
4. **Run the numbers on realitycents.com.** Use the rent vs. buy calculator and other tools built for the Hawaii market. Use these numbers to help you determine a good ballpark price range with a payment that is comfortable.

5. **If you're keeping a current property as a rental, get a lease.** If you're PCS'ing to Hawaii and plan to rent out your current home, start working on securing a tenant and a signed 12-month lease. That lease is the documentation you'll need to use the 75% rental income offset — which can dramatically improve your qualification picture.
6. **Know your TLA benefit.** If you're PCS'ing to Hawaii, you're entitled to 30 days of Temporary Living Allowance (extendable to 60 with a signed purchase agreement). Factor this into your timeline — it gives you breathing room to find the right home without rushing.

# 7

# THE HAWAII REAL ESTATE LANDSCAPE

Welcome to Part III — where we shift from VA loans in general to Hawaii specifically. Hawaii's real estate market operates by its own rules. Property types, legal structures, and financing mechanisms differ fundamentally from the mainland — and if you approach it like buying a home in Texas or North Carolina, you'll get tripped up.

This chapter covers the landscape: property types you'll encounter, unique legal distinctions, and what you need to understand before shopping.

## FEE SIMPLE VS. LEASEHOLD — HAWAII'S MOST UNIQUE DISTINCTION

Fee simple vs. leasehold is the core distinction separating Hawaii real estate from everywhere else in the country. If you take nothing else from this chapter, take this:

## Fee Simple

Fee simple means you own both land and building — complete ownership. You pay property taxes and maintenance, and the property is yours to sell, lease, or pass down. This is what you want.

## Leasehold

Leasehold is different: you own the building or unit but not the land underneath. You lease the land from a landowner and pay lease rent in addition to your mortgage.

Why? Hawaii's large landowners — Bishop Estate (Kamehameha Schools), Queen Liliuokalani Trust, and Hawaiian trusts — historically held vast tracts and leased rather than sold. While many properties have converted to fee simple, leasehold still exists throughout the islands.

The problem: lease rent renegotiation can double or triple your monthly housing costs overnight, fundamentally changing your housing economics. As lease terms shorten, properties become harder to sell and finance. Leasehold properties typically sell at significant discounts compared to fee simple, and for good reason — the discount reflects the real financial risk of escalating lease rents, declining property values as the lease term shortens, and significant difficulty reselling.

Where will you encounter leasehold? It's most common in certain Waikiki towers, parts of Hawaii Kai, some Kailua and Kaneohe properties, and scattered throughout Oahu wherever large trusts or estates held land historically. You'll also find leasehold on the Big Island, Maui, and Kauai. The listings don't always make it obvious — the price catches your eye first, and the land tenure is buried in the details. That's why you always check before getting emotionally attached to a property.

> **Jay's Pro Tip:** "Here's my bottom line on leasehold: avoid it in 98% of cases. When you see a Hawaii listing that looks 'too good to be true'

— priced well below comparable properties — check the land tenure. It's almost always leasehold, and that discounted price is there for a reason. While VA loans can technically be used for qualifying leasehold properties, the requirements are strict and the scenarios where leasehold makes financial sense are exceedingly rare. Stick with fee simple. When you're searching listings, look for the letters 'FS' (fee simple) and steer clear of 'LH' (leasehold). Your agent and your lender should both be confirming this on every property you consider."

## CONDOS VS. SINGLE-FAMILY HOMES VS. TOWNHOMES

On Oahu, condos dominate the market. Land is scarce, expensive, and often protected. Condominiums represent the primary entry point for most homebuyers, including military families. Hawaii condos range from modest walk-ups in Aiea to modern high-rises in Kakaako with ocean views and resort-style amenities. Many service members buy condos in Ewa Beach, Kapolei, or Mililani and find them to be a perfect fit for their needs and budget.

Single-family homes cost a premium. On Oahu, median prices exceed $900,000, with neighborhoods like Kailua, Hawaii Kai, and the North Shore pushing higher. For many service members, single-family homes become realistic later in their career — after building equity through condo purchases — or in less expensive island areas.

Townhomes occupy the middle ground: more space than a condo with a small yard, but typically with HOA and shared structural elements. They're a good option for families wanting more room without the single-family price tag.

### CPR — Condominium Property Regime

CPR (Condominium Property Regime), governed by Hawaii Revised Statutes Chapter 514B, is a unique Hawaii legal mechanism that allows a single property to be divided into two or more separately-owned units with shared common elements. Each CPR unit receives its own fee simple deed and its own separate TMK (Tax Map Key) number.

CPR is not the same as subdivision — it cannot change zoning, building restrictions, or usage rules. But it does create individually-owned units that can be bought and sold separately. You'll encounter CPR properties throughout Hawaii — sometimes a house that's been split into two units, sometimes a duplex where each unit has its own deed.

Here's a concrete example: you're touring what looks like a single-family house in Kailua — detached, private yard, no shared walls. But when you pull the deed, it says "CPR Unit A." What does that mean for you? It means the original property was legally divided into two or more units under Hawaii's CPR statute. Your "house" is actually one unit of a multi-unit CPR. You'll likely have shared common elements (driveway, utility connections, possibly structural components), governing documents similar to a condo association, and potential VA project approval requirements.

The distinction matters for lending, insurance, appraisal, and VA eligibility. CPR-created units may require condo-type VA project approval depending on how they're structured, even if the property looks and feels like a standalone house. Your lender and your agent should be checking this on every property.

## MULTI-FAMILY AND MULTI-GENERATIONAL PROPERTIES

### Multi-Generational and Ohana Properties

Hawaii has a long tradition of multi-generational living. It's deeply rooted in Hawaiian and Pacific Islander culture — the concept of ohana (family) extends to how people live, with multiple generations sharing a single property. You'll see this reflected throughout the islands in properties with ohana units, converted garages, enclosed lanais that have become bedrooms, and Accessory Dwelling Units (ADUs).

This creates a unique situation for homebuyers. You might tour a single-family listing and find two or three separate living spaces. The appeal is obvious — extra space, potential rental income, room for extended family. Important lending considerations apply.

Here's the critical financing reality: unless a property is legally zoned and permitted as a multi-family dwelling (duplex, triplex, or fourplex), it must be financed as a single-family home — regardless of how many separate living spaces it actually contains. That means if you're buying a house with an ohana unit, a converted garage apartment, and a cottage in the backyard, the lender treats it as a single-family purchase. No consideration is given to potential rental income from those extra spaces when qualifying you for the loan. You must qualify based on your own income and debts alone.

Only properties legally zoned and permitted as 2–4 unit multi-family dwellings can be financed as multi-family, with rental income from non-owner-occupied units used for qualifying. Many buyers mentally add rental income from extra spaces — but unless the property has legal multi-family designation, that income doesn't count.

## Permitted vs. Unpermitted Areas

Many of Hawaii's additional living spaces were built without permits. That converted garage, the enclosed lanai, the "cottage" in the backyard — unless they went through the county permitting process, they're unpermitted.

Here's what this means for VA lending: the VA appraiser will note unpermitted additions and will not give value to unpermitted square footage or structures. However — and this is good news — this usually does not create complications for the loan itself. The appraiser simply excludes the unpermitted area from the valuation. The property can still be financed; you just won't get credit for the extra space in the appraised value.

Why does this matter? Because it affects what you're really paying for. If a property is listed at $800,000 and part of the appeal is a beautiful converted garage that's now a guest suite, the VA appraisal won't include that space in the valuation. If the appraised value comes in lower than the purchase price because of excluded unpermitted areas, you and your agent need to factor that into your offer strategy.

> **By the Book:** Per VA Pamphlet 26-7, Chapter 7 (Loans Requiring Special Underwriting), the VA allows loans on 1–4 unit properties, but the veteran must occupy one unit as their primary residence. For true multi-family properties (legally zoned and permitted), rental income from the non-owner-occupied units can be used for qualifying, with specific VA requirements for income and expense calculations. But remember: a single-family home with unpermitted extra units is NOT a multi-family property in the eyes of the lender or the VA — it's a single-family home, period.

## CONDOTELS AND SHORT-TERM RENTALS

At some point during your house search, you're going to see a condo listed in or near Waikiki at what seems like an attractive price, and you're going to think: "I could live there AND rent it out on Airbnb when I'm not using it." Let me save you some time and heartache.

A condotel is a hotel-condo hybrid — a property that operates as part of a hotel, where individual units can be privately owned but are often part of a rental pool managed by the hotel. They're common in Waikiki and resort areas throughout the islands. They're also, in almost every case, not eligible for VA financing.

There are two reasons for this. First, the VA requires that the property be the veteran's primary residence. A condotel that's part of a hotel rental pool is fundamentally designed as an investment or vacation property, not a primary residence. Second, most condotel projects do not meet VA condo approval standards — their governance structures, insurance arrangements, and commercial use ratios typically don't align with what the VA requires.

Beyond condotels, you should also know that Honolulu and other

Hawaii counties have strict regulations on vacation rentals outside designated resort zones. Operating an unpermitted short-term rental (less than 30 days) in most residential areas of Oahu is illegal and subject to significant fines. The county has been actively enforcing these rules.

If your homebuying plan involves generating short-term rental income, make sure you understand the regulations for the specific area you're buying in. Your real estate agent should be able to tell you whether a property is in a zone where short-term rentals are permitted. In most residential neighborhoods, they're not.

> **Hawaii Insider:** "Every year service members ask about buying a Waikiki condo and Airbnbing it when deployed. The lending reality and legal landscape make this extremely difficult with a VA loan. If short-term rental income is your strategy, you'll need conventional financing, a properly zoned area, and a separate investment — not a VA-financed primary residence."

## THE BOTTOM LINE

Hawaii's real estate market operates by its own rules. Fee simple vs. leasehold, CPR vs. true single-family, permitted vs. unpermitted, VA-approved condos vs. everything else — these distinctions don't exist in most mainland markets, and they have real implications for your financing, your property value, and your long-term investment.

The good news is that none of this is complicated once you understand it. And now you do. In the next chapter, we'll dive deep into one of the most important topics for Hawaii VA buyers: the condo approval process, HOA considerations, and the insurance landscape.

## ACTION ITEMS

1. **Learn to spot leasehold listings.** When browsing Hawaii real estate listings, always check the land tenure. Look for "FS" (fee simple) or "LH" (leasehold). If the price seems too good to be true, it's almost certainly leasehold. Make it a habit to verify before you get attached to a property.
2. **Understand the property type before you tour.** Is it a true single-family home, a CPR unit, a condo, or a townhome? The answer affects financing, insurance, VA approval requirements, and your monthly costs. Your agent should clarify this on every property.
3. **Check for unpermitted additions and understand the financing implications.** If a property has extra living spaces — converted garages, enclosed lanais, additional units — ask whether they're permitted. The VA appraiser won't give value to unpermitted areas, which can affect the appraised value and your offer strategy. And remember: unless the property is legally zoned and permitted as a multi-family dwelling, it will be financed as a single-family home with no rental income consideration for qualifying.
4. **Skip the condotel dream (for now).** If you're buying with a VA loan, condotels and short-term rental properties in hotel zones are almost certainly off the table. Focus your search on fee simple condos in VA-approved projects or single-family homes — that's where your VA benefit works best.
5. **Check VA condo approval status.** Before falling in love with a condo, check the VA's condo approval database at lgy.va.gov/lgyhub/condo-report. If the project isn't approved, don't panic — your lender may be able to pursue approval — but it's better to know upfront than to discover it after you've made an offer.

# 8

# THE CONDO CONUNDRUM — VA APPROVAL AND HAWAII HOAS

If you're buying a condo in Hawaii with a VA loan — and statistically you likely are — this chapter covers the layer that doesn't exist when buying a single-family home: the condo project itself must be VA-approved.

Not the unit. The entire building or complex must be certified by the VA before any lender can originate a VA loan for a unit in that project. This is the single biggest source of confusion and missed opportunities for VA buyers in Hawaii — and it's where having the right lender makes the most dramatic difference.

## VA CONDO PROJECT APPROVAL

### How It Works

Per VA Pamphlet 26-7, Chapter 16, condominiums must receive full VA project approval before a VA loan can be originated for any unit in that project. The VA reviews the project as a whole — its finances, insurance, governance, and legal standing — to ensure it meets minimum standards.

This is different from the appraisal of your individual unit. Even if your unit is pristine — excellent condition, great location, fair price — you cannot close a VA loan on it if the project hasn't been approved.

An important note: VA condo approvals do not expire. Once a project is approved, it stays approved unless something changes. However, approvals can be suspended or revoked. If significant structural defects, soil erosion, or similar issues threaten the building, the VA will suspend approval. For less severe issues — such as a 'slip-and-fall' lawsuit against the HOA — the VA may update status from "Accepted Without Conditions" to "Accepted With Conditions." In that case, your lender can still approve a VA loan, but the veteran must sign a letter acknowledging the issue and accepting the property as-is.

## How to Check Approval Status

The VA maintains a live condo approval database at lgy.va.gov/lgyhub/condo-report. Look for "Accepted Without Conditions" — that means the project is currently VA-approved and you're clear to proceed. You may also see "Accepted With Conditions," which means the project is approved but there's a minor issue requiring acknowledgment.

A practical tip for searching: use state searches only and the fewest characters possible in the project name. The database is finicky with spelling — if you type the name slightly differently than registered, you'll get no results. For example, searching "Ahakea at Hoopili" (without the apostrophe, known as the 'okina' in Hawaii) returns nothing. The full project name is Ahakea at Ho'opili but searching just "Ahakea" alone works. Fewer characters, broader search.

The good news: Oahu alone has over 800 VA-approved condo projects. Many popular buildings — including highly desirable complexes in Kaka'ako and Waikiki — are NOT yet approved, but may be approvable with the right documentation.

## What the VA Reviews

When evaluating a condo project, the VA examines:

**Association finances.** Is the HOA financially healthy? Are reserves adequately funded? A high delinquency rate on HOA dues is a red flag.

**Insurance adequacy.** Does the master policy meet federal lending requirements? This has become increasingly important in Hawaii.

**Governance structure.** Is the association properly organized? Are board meetings held and documents in order?

**Owner-occupancy ratios.** What percentage of units are owner-occupied versus investor-owned rentals?

**Litigation status.** Is the association involved in active lawsuits, particularly construction defect claims?

**Commercial space ratios.** How much of the project is commercial versus residential?

## Common Reasons Projects Fail

The most common obstacles include insufficient insurance coverage, too much commercial space, delinquent HOA dues rates exceeding thresholds, and pending litigation against the association.

## This Is Where Your Lender Matters Most

An experienced VA lender will obtain and submit all necessary documents to pursue full VA project approval for any unapproved condo you're interested in — provided the project qualifies under VA guidelines. Many condos that aren't currently VA-approved CAN be approved with the right documentation and an experienced lender driving the process.

If you find a condo you love that isn't on the VA-approved list, don't walk away before your lender evaluates whether approval is achievable. A good VA lender can review the project documents, identify potential issues, and give you a realistic assessment of timing and feasibility.

> **Jay's Pro Tip:** "I've gotten dozens of condo projects VA-approved over the years that weren't on the list when my client first found the unit. Here's how we handle it: we always check VA condo approval status before issuing a pre-approval letter — remember, our pre-approval letters are property-specific. If the condo looks approvable but isn't yet approved, we get the buyer into contract, then submit the paperwork to the Regional VA office for approval. We can typically get the condo approved and still close within a standard 45-day closing timeline. It takes some work — gathering the HOA financials, insurance certificates, governing documents, and submitting the full package — but it's absolutely doable when the project is fundamentally sound."
>
> **From the Closing Table: The Condo Approval That Closed in 38 Days**
>
> An Air Force Captain found a two-bedroom unit in a Kaneohe building that wasn't on the VA-approved list. Her agent told her to move on — "It'll take months to get approved." She called me anyway. We pulled the HOA financials, the master insurance certificate, the governing documents, and the reserve study. The building was fundamentally sound — good reserves, adequate insurance, proper governance, reasonable owner-occupancy ratio. I submitted the full approval package to the VA Regional Loan Center on day 3 of escrow. The VA issued approval on day 18. We closed on day 38. The Captain moved in with her family that weekend. Don't assume a condo that isn't on the list can't be approved. Ask your lender to evaluate it first. The answer might surprise you.

## HOA DUES AND MAINTENANCE FEES

### What Your HOA Fees Actually Cover

If you're coming from the mainland, where HOA fees of $50–$150/month are standard, Hawaii's fees will look very different. Hawaii condo HOAs typically cover far more: water and sewer, trash removal, the building's master insurance policy, maintenance of common areas (lobbies, hallways, elevators, parking, pools, recreation areas), landscaping, building management, and contributions to the reserve fund.

That's why Hawaii HOA fees tend to be higher — many expenses that would be separate bills in a single-family home are bundled into your HOA fee.

### Typical Fee Ranges

HOA fees in Honolulu vary widely by building type, age, amenities, and location. Basic low-rise buildings with minimal amenities run $300–$400/month. Mid-range buildings with pools and fitness centers run $500–$800/month. Luxury high-rises with concierge, resort-style amenities, and full security can exceed $1,000–$1,500/month.

A condo with a low purchase price but a $1,000/month HOA fee may cost as much as a more expensive condo with a $400/month fee.

### How HOA Fees Affect Your Qualification

Per VA underwriting guidelines, the full HOA fee is added to your monthly housing obligation when calculating your DTI. Your total housing payment is PITI (principal, interest, taxes, insurance) plus HOA. A $700/month HOA fee has the exact same impact on your debt-to-income ratio as $700/month in car payments.

This surprises many buyers. You might qualify comfortably for a certain purchase price, but adding a $650 or $800 HOA fee on top of

PITI moves your DTI into a different zone. Always factor the HOA into your affordability analysis from the beginning.

## Reserve Studies and HOA Financial Health

Before buying a condo, review the association's financials — specifically the reserve study and current financial statements. Look for:

**The reserve fund.** How much money does the association have in reserves for major capital repairs — roof replacement, elevator modernization, plumbing upgrades, exterior painting? A well-funded reserve means the association can handle these expenses without hitting owners with surprise assessments.

**The funding ratio.** What percentage of the recommended reserve balance does the association actually have? Above 70% is generally healthy. Below 50% is a warning sign that the association may be underfunded and a special assessment is likely.

**Special assessments.** Has the association levied recent special assessments? Are any planned? These one-time charges to unit owners cover major expenses the reserve fund can't handle — and they can be five- or six-figure amounts for elevator replacements, plumbing overhauls, or concrete restoration on aging high-rises.

## Red Flags in HOA Documents

Keep an eye out for: significantly underfunded reserves (below 50%), pending litigation against the association (especially construction defect claims), high delinquency rates on HOA dues, recent large special assessments, and rapidly increasing HOA fees.

> **Hawaii Insider:** "Here's something I always tell my clients: don't just look at the condo — look at the building. A beautiful unit in a poorly managed building is a ticking time bomb. Read the board meeting minutes. Look at the reserve study. Ask about upcoming capital projects. The best condo purchase is one where the unit is in good

condition AND the building is financially healthy and well-managed."

## HAWAII'S CONDO INSURANCE LANDSCAPE

This section deserves special attention because the condo insurance market in Hawaii has been significantly disrupted in recent years, directly affecting VA buyers.

### What Happened

Starting in late 2023, Hawaii condo association master policy premiums saw dramatic increases — some associations experienced 300% or more in a single renewal year. The Lahaina wildfire in August 2023 added enormous pressure to an already tightening market. Several national insurance carriers pulled back from Hawaii coverage or significantly reduced their exposure.

### Where Things Stand Now

The good news: these issues are gradually resolving. State legislation — specifically Act 296, signed into law in July 2025 — has provided regulatory relief. The reinsurance market is stabilizing. Some buildings are already seeing 15–20% decreases in premiums, though rates generally remain above pre-2023 levels. This is an issue being addressed, not an ongoing crisis.

### Why It Matters for VA Buyers

Underinsured condo projects can fail federal lending requirements, meaning they can temporarily lose eligibility for VA financing. If a building's master policy doesn't provide adequate coverage, the VA won't approve the project, and your loan can't close.

Work with an experienced VA lender who can evaluate a project's insurance health before you make an offer. A good lender will check the building's master policy coverage levels, confirm the coverage meets VA requirements, and flag any potential issues before they become deal-breakers.

### What VA Lenders Require

For condo projects, VA lenders must verify that the association's master policy provides adequate coverage — typically replacement cost coverage for the building's common elements and structure. This includes adequate hazard insurance, fidelity bond coverage to protect against financial mismanagement, and flood insurance if the project is in a designated flood zone.

### How to Evaluate a Project's Insurance Health

When considering a condo, ask: What is the current master policy coverage level? Has the association experienced significant premium increases in the past two years? Does the coverage meet replacement cost thresholds? Is there adequate fidelity bond coverage? Has the building had difficulty securing or renewing its insurance?

The answers will tell you whether the building is on solid ground from an insurance perspective — and whether your VA loan is likely to encounter issues related to the project's insurance.

## THE BOTTOM LINE

Buying a condo in Hawaii with a VA loan adds an extra layer of complexity — project approval, HOA analysis, and insurance verification — that doesn't exist with single-family homes. But it's absolutely manageable with the right lender and approach. Over 800 condo projects on Oahu alone are VA-approved, and many more can be approved when an experienced lender drives the process.

The key is doing your homework: check VA approval status before getting emotionally invested, factor HOA fees into affordability calculations from day one, review the association's financial health, and ensure the building's insurance is adequate. These steps protect you from surprises and set you up for a smooth closing and sound investment.

## ACTION ITEMS

1. **Check the VA condo database.** Look it up at lgy.va.gov/lgyhub/condo-report before getting attached. Search by state and use as few characters as possible in the project name. Look for "Accepted Without Conditions" or "Accepted With Conditions." If the project shows "Suspended," ask your lender what that means.
2. **Factor HOA fees into your budget from the start.** When browsing listings, always check the monthly HOA fee. Add it to your estimated PITI to get your true monthly housing cost. A $550,000 condo with $900 HOA feels very different from one with $400 HOA.
3. **Request HOA documents before you commit.** Ask for the most recent reserve study, financial statements, board meeting minutes, and information about planned special assessments or capital projects. Your agent can help obtain these during due diligence.
4. **Ask about insurance.** Have your agent or lender confirm that the building's master policy meets current coverage requirements. Ask about recent premium changes and renewal difficulties.
5. **Don't walk away from an unapproved condo too quickly.** If you find a unit you love in a building that isn't VA-approved, tell your lender before giving up. The project may be perfectly eligible — it just hasn't been submitted. An experienced VA lender can get the buyer into contract, submit approval paperwork, and typically close within a standard 45-day timeline.

# 9

# INSURING YOUR PARADISE — HOMEOWNER'S INSURANCE IN HAWAII

Insurance is one of the most important — and most misunderstood — aspects of buying in Hawaii. The insurance landscape differs significantly from the mainland, requirements vary by property type, and the market has faced real turbulence in recent years. This chapter covers what coverage you need, how it differs for single-family homes versus condos, and how to navigate Hawaii's unique market.

## SINGLE-FAMILY HOME INSURANCE

### What a Standard Policy Covers

Single-family homes require a standard homeowner's insurance policy (HO-3) covering the structure, personal property, liability protection, and additional living expenses if uninhabitable due to a covered event. The basic framework mirrors mainland policies but with Hawaii-specific considerations.

## Hurricane and Windstorm Coverage

Hawaii is in a hurricane zone, and many standard homeowner's policies exclude or limit windstorm and hurricane damage. While direct hurricane hits are relatively rare — Hurricane Iniki devastated Kauai in 1992, and tropical storms periodically threaten the islands — the risk is real and your lender will require adequate coverage.

For most Hawaii home buyers, hurricane coverage is obtained through a private carrier, either bundled into a comprehensive homeowners policy or as a standalone endorsement. The Hawaii Hurricane Relief Fund (HHRF), established after Iniki as a last-resort option, remains available but is rarely used for single-family home purchases today — private market options are generally more accessible and competitively priced. The cost of coverage varies based on your property's location, construction type, and proximity to the coast. Expect a meaningful addition to your annual insurance bill, but it's a non-negotiable part of responsible homeownership in the islands.

Make sure you understand exactly what your base homeowner's policy covers and what it excludes. Some policies include wind damage but exclude "named storms" or hurricane-force winds specifically. Others exclude windstorm entirely. Don't assume — read the policy or have your insurance broker walk you through it. Your VA lender requires adequate hazard insurance covering all major perils, and a gap in hurricane coverage could delay your closing.

## Flood Insurance

If your property is in a FEMA-designated flood zone, flood insurance is required — your lender won't close the loan without it. But even if your property isn't in a high-risk flood zone, flood insurance can be smart to have. Hawaii experiences heavy rain events, flash flooding, and coastal surge, and standard homeowner's policies do not cover flood damage. Flood insurance is available through the National Flood Insurance Program (NFIP) and through private carriers. Rates vary significantly based on your flood zone designation, elevation, and the property's construction. Your insurance agent can help you determine whether flood coverage is required and what it will cost.

## Lava Zone Considerations

This one is primarily relevant to Big Island buyers, but it's worth knowing even if you're focused on Oahu — because the insurance dynamics illustrate how Hawaii's natural environment affects the market in ways the mainland simply doesn't.

The Big Island of Hawaii has active volcanic zones, and the USGS classifies areas into lava zones 1 through 9, with 1 being highest risk. Properties in lava zones 1 and 2 — the areas most directly in the path of potential lava flows — can be extremely difficult or impossible to insure through conventional carriers. After the 2018 Kilauea eruption, which destroyed over 700 homes in Leilani Estates (a lava zone 1 area), several carriers exited the Big Island market or dramatically increased premiums in high-risk zones.

If you're considering a Big Island property, check the lava zone designation before you get attached. Properties in zones 1 and 2 may require specialty insurance at significantly higher premiums — if coverage is available at all. Some areas may effectively be uninsurable through standard markets, which creates an obvious problem for VA financing: your lender requires adequate hazard insurance to close. No insurance means no loan.

Properties in lower-risk zones (3–9) are generally insurable through standard carriers, though premiums may still reflect the Big Island's volcanic classification. For the vast majority of military homebuyers focused on Oahu, lava zones are not a concern — Oahu has no active volcanic risk. But if your house hunt takes you to the neighbor islands, this is something to research early and discuss with both your insurance broker and your lender.

### What VA Lenders Require

In Hawaii, lenders require hazard insurance that covers 100% of the replacement cost of the entire dwelling — enough to completely rebuild the home if it's destroyed by fire or another covered event. This isn't "loan balance or replacement cost, whichever is less" — it's full replacement cost, period. Your lender will verify this as part of the closing process, and the policy must be in place and paid through at least the first year before closing.

## CONDO INSURANCE (HO-6)

Condo insurance in Hawaii works differently from single-family home insurance because there are two layers of coverage: the association's master policy and your personal unit-owner's policy (known as an HO-6). Understanding the difference between these two layers — and what each one covers — is essential.

### The Master Policy: What Your Association Covers

The condo association carries a master insurance policy that covers the building as a whole. But not all master policies are created equal, and the type of coverage determines what falls on you as the unit owner. There are three types you should know about:

**"Walls-in" coverage** — The standard in 99.9% of Hawaii high-rise condos and townhomes. The association's master policy covers the building's exterior, common areas, and typically interior walls, floors, and original fixtures. Your HO-6 covers your personal property, upgrades or improvements, and personal liability.

**"All-in" coverage** — Rare, primarily in CPR (Condominium Property Regime) projects. These are properties that look and function like a standalone house but are technically classified as condominiums. They typically have little to no association dues, the master policy doesn't provide insurance, and you insure the entire dwelling yourself like a traditional single-family home. Confirm coverage details if buying a CPR property.

**"Bare walls" coverage** — Covers only the structural shell; everything inside (walls, flooring, fixtures, appliances, personal property) is your responsibility. Uncommon in Hawaii, but confirm what your association's policy actually covers.

## Your HO-6 Policy: What You Need

Your HO-6 policy is your personal condo insurance, and you need one regardless of whether your unit has been upgraded or not. Pretty much every condo purchase requires an HO-6 policy. The only exception is buying a brand-new unit directly from the developer — and even then, an HO-6 is still recommended because the master policy doesn't cover your personal property or liability.

For a walls-in building (the standard), your HO-6 should cover: your personal property (furniture, electronics, clothing, everything you own inside the unit), any upgrades or improvements you've made (renovated kitchen, new flooring, upgraded bathroom), your personal liability (if someone is injured in your unit), and additional living expenses (if your unit becomes uninhabitable due to a covered event).

## Loss Assessment Coverage — Don't Skip This

Loss assessment coverage is often overlooked but can save tens of thousands of dollars. If a disaster damages common areas and the master policy doesn't fully cover repairs, the association can levy special assessments against all unit owners. Loss assessment coverage on your HO-6 protects you from those assessments — typically just a few dollars a month for $25,000–$100,000 in coverage. With high building repair costs, this is one of the smartest insurance dollars you can spend.

## How the Master Policy and HO-6 Work Together

Understanding the interaction between the two layers prevents both gaps and unnecessary overlap. When the master policy is walls-in (the standard), the association covers the building shell, common areas, and typically original interior finishes. Your HO-6 picks up where the master policy stops — covering your personal belongings, any upgrades or improvements, your personal liability, and additional living expenses.

Here's a scenario that illustrates why both layers matter: a pipe bursts in the wall of your unit, flooding your kitchen. The master policy covers the repair of the pipe and the wall itself (building infrastructure). Your HO-6 covers your damaged personal property (furniture, electronics, clothing) and any upgrades you made (the granite countertops, the new flooring). Without the HO-6, you're paying out of pocket for everything inside your unit. Without adequate master policy coverage, the building repair costs get assessed to all unit owners.

The key question to ask when evaluating any condo purchase: does the master policy's coverage type (walls-in, all-in, or bare walls) align with what your HO-6 covers? There should be no gap between where one policy ends and the other begins. Your insurance agent can review both policies and confirm there's no gap.

## What VA Lenders Require for Your HO-6

Your VA lender will require that your HO-6 coverage is adequate to protect the lender's interest in the property. For most condo units, $25,000 to $50,000 in dwelling coverage is sufficient to cover the gap between the master policy and full replacement of your unit's interior. If your unit has been substantially upgraded — a full kitchen remodel, high-end flooring, custom bathrooms — you may want to carry more dwelling coverage to reflect the added value of those improvements. Your insurance agent can help you determine the right amount based on your specific unit and the master policy's coverage.

## THE INSURANCE LANDSCAPE IN HAWAII

### Why the Market Has Been Challenging

Hawaii's insurance market has faced challenges: several national carriers pulled out or reduced coverage. Factors include geographic isolation, the Lahaina wildfire's impact on reinsurance costs, aging Oahu building stock requiring higher coverage, and national trends toward reducing exposure in high-risk coastal markets. This means limited options and higher premiums than the mainland, but state legislation and normalizing reinsurance are gradually improving conditions.

### The Hawaii Property Insurance Association (HPIA)

If you can't find coverage through standard carriers, the Hawaii Property Insurance Association (HPIA) serves as an insurer of last resort, providing basic property insurance for homeowners unable to obtain private market coverage. Coverage is more limited and premiums higher than commercial policies, but it ensures you meet lender requirements.

### Shopping for Competitive Rates

Practical tips for navigating Hawaii's insurance market:

**Work with a local insurance broker.** A Hawaii-based broker who knows the local market can often find better rates than shopping national carriers online. They know which companies are actively writing policies in Hawaii, which offer the best rates for specific property types, and how to package coverage to minimize your costs.

**Bundle your policies.** If you can get your auto insurance, HO-6 or homeowner's policy, and umbrella coverage through the same carrier, you'll typically receive a multi-policy discount. This is one of the easiest ways to reduce your overall insurance costs.

**Consider your deductible.** A higher deductible means a lower premium. If you have sufficient reserves to cover a $2,500 or $5,000 deductible out of pocket, raising your deductible from $1,000 can meaningfully reduce your annual premium.

**Ask about mitigation credits.** Some carriers offer discounts for hurricane-resistant construction features, security systems, fire alarms, or other risk-reducing measures. If your home or building has these features, make sure your carrier knows.

**Jay's Pro Tip:** "Don't wait until the last minute to shop for insurance. Start getting quotes as soon as you go under contract — not the week before closing. Hawaii's insurance market can take longer to navigate than the mainland, and you don't want a delay in securing coverage to hold up your closing. Your lender needs proof of insurance before they can issue final approval of your loan. Line it up early and it's one less thing to worry about."

## THE BOTTOM LINE

Insurance in Hawaii requires more attention than most mainland markets. Whether you're buying a single-family home or a condo, you need to understand what coverage is required, what the master policy does and doesn't cover, and how to navigate a market that's been through some turbulence. The good news: insurance is a solvable problem — with the right broker, right coverage, and a proactive approach, you can protect your investment without breaking the bank.

Address insurance when you go under contract, not at closing. It's one of the easiest parts of the transaction to get right — and one of the costliest to get wrong.

## ACTION ITEMS

1. **Determine your coverage type early.** If you're buying a single-family home or CPR property, plan for full homeowner's insurance with 100% replacement cost coverage — enough to completely rebuild the home — plus hurricane/windstorm coverage. If you're buying a condo, find out what type of master policy the building carries (walls-in, all-in, or bare walls) so you know what your HO-6 needs to cover.
2. **Get an HO-6 policy for any condo purchase.** Whether upgraded or not, you need an HO-6 policy. Most units require $25,000–$50,000 in dwelling coverage; more if substantially upgraded. Your HO-6 also covers personal property, liability, and additional living expenses.
3. **Add loss assessment coverage to your HO-6.** This affordable add-on protects you from special assessments after a building-wide disaster. Ask your agent about $50,000–$100,000 in coverage — it typically costs just a few dollars monthly.
4. **Get insurance quotes as soon as you go under contract.** Start shopping early for your HO-6 or HO-3 homeowner's policy to lock in competitive rates before your lender needs proof. Work with a local Hawaii insurance broker — they often find better rates and options than online shopping.
5. **Confirm flood zone status.** Check whether your property is in a FEMA-designated flood zone. If yes, flood insurance is required. Even if not, consider whether location warrants coverage as additional protection.

# 10

# MONEY MATTERS — CLOSING COSTS, ESCROW, AND HAWAII'S UNIQUE TIMELINES

"Zero down" doesn't mean "zero cost." Your VA loan finances 100% of the purchase price, but closing costs, prepaids, and escrow deposits still require cash — and Hawaii's process differs significantly from the mainland. If you come in expecting a mainland-style closing, you'll be confused and possibly scrambling at the last minute. This chapter covers what to expect financially, how Hawaii's escrow works, the extended closing timeline, and Hawaii's favorable property tax system.

## UNDERSTANDING CLOSING COSTS IN HAWAII

### What You'll Actually Pay

Plan for 1.5–2% of the purchase price in closing costs. On a typical Hawaii VA purchase, this includes VA appraisal, lender fees, title insurance (lender's and owner's policies), escrow fees, recording fees to the State of Hawaii Bureau of Conveyances, and discount points if you choose to buy down your rate.

Prepaids also require cash at closing: your first year of homeowner's insurance (or HO-6 for condos), prepaid property taxes (typically a few months' worth to fund your impound account), and prepaid interest from loan funding through month-end. On a $600,000 purchase, total cash needed at closing runs $9,000–$12,000 — a fraction of the 3–5% down payment plus closing costs conventional buyers need to bring.

## VA Closing Cost Rules — What You Can and Can't Pay

Per VA Pamphlet 26-7, Chapter 8, veterans can pay customary closing costs including appraisal, credit report, title insurance, escrow fees, recording fees, and discount points. The 1% origination fee triggers VA "non-allowable fee" restrictions, meaning document preparation, processing, and underwriting fees cannot also be charged. Most Hawaii lenders avoid this by charging itemized fees (processing, underwriting) totaling around $2,000 instead. A 1% origination on a $600,000 loan would be $6,000 but restrict additional charges — so itemized fees work better for borrowers. Your lender must ensure all charges comply with VA guidelines.

## The VA Funding Fee at Closing

The funding fee is unique to VA loans: 2.15% for first-time use, 3.30% for subsequent use. It can be financed into your loan balance. If you have a 10%+ VA disability rating or are a Purple Heart recipient, you're exempt — saving nearly $13,000 on a $600,000 loan. The funding fee is also tax-deductible as a mortgage insurance premium on Schedule A; consult your tax professional.

## Can the Seller Pay Your Closing Costs?

The VA caps "seller concessions" at 4% of purchase price, but here's the key: normal closing costs and discount points don't count toward that cap. The 4% limit applies only to non-closing-cost items (debt payoff, gifts). A seller can cover closing costs, prepaids, and buy down your rate — potentially tens of thousands — as long as non-closing-cost concessions stay within 4%. In hot markets, sellers resist; in balanced markets, they're standard. Your agent will advise what's realistic.

> **Jay's Pro Tip:** "Here's a move I recommend to buyers who are tight on cash: instead of asking the seller for a lower price, ask them to contribute toward your closing costs at the full asking price. The seller gets their number, and you preserve your cash. On a $600,000 purchase, $10,000 in seller concessions covers most or all of your closing costs — and that $10,000 barely affects the seller's net proceeds after commissions and other selling expenses. It's often an easier 'yes' than a price reduction."

## HAWAII'S ESCROW PROCESS — IT'S NOT LIKE THE MAINLAND

### Hawaii Is an Escrow State

Hawaii is an escrow state — a neutral third-party escrow company manages the closing process. The escrow officer coordinates between buyer, seller, lender, and agents to ensure documents are signed, funds are collected and distributed, and the transaction records with the State of Hawaii. Think of escrow as the air traffic controller for your transaction: they work for the deal, not either side.

### The Typical Escrow Timeline

A standard Hawaii VA purchase closes within 30–45 days from escrow opening (when your offer is accepted and contract is executed). Here's the flow:

**Days 1–5:** Escrow opens. Your initial earnest money deposit — typically $1,000 (up to $5,000) — is delivered to the escrow company. You schedule your home inspection right away. Here's a critical detail: do not order the VA appraisal yet. The $900 fee falls on you if the deal collapses during inspection. Clear the inspection first.

**Days 5–15:** The home inspection is completed. After you and the seller agree on inspection terms, you sign off on Paragraph J-1 of the purchase agreement — the formal acknowledgment that the inspection contingency is satisfied. Once J-1 is signed, two things happen: you make a subsequent earnest money deposit to escrow (typically another $1,000 to $5,000 or more) and your lender orders the VA appraisal. Both deposits credit toward your final cash to close. Title search and preliminary title report are also prepared during this time.

> **Jay's Pro Tip:** "I always wait until the home inspection is completed and J-1 is signed off before ordering the appraisal. That $900 appraisal fee could be the buyer's responsibility if the deal falls through due to inspection issues. There's no reason to put a Veteran at risk for that cost when we can clear the inspection contingency first and still have plenty of time for the appraisal. Protecting my clients' money at every step is part of the job."

**Days 15–30:** The VA appraisal is in process (this can take 7–14 days in Hawaii due to limited VA-approved appraiser availability on the islands). Your lender completes underwriting and issues a "clear to close." Final loan documents are prepared and sent to escrow. You do your final walkthrough of the property.

**Days 30–35:** You sign loan documents at the escrow office (or with a mobile notary). Your lender reviews the signed documents and then wires the loan funds to escrow.

**Days 35–40:** This is where Hawaii gets different:

## Delayed Funding and Recording — The #1 Thing Mainland Buyers Don't Understand

On the mainland, "closing day" usually means you sign papers, the loan funds, and you get your keys — all on the same day. In Hawaii, it does not work this way.

The actual closing date in Hawaii is when the transaction officially records with the State of Hawaii Bureau of Conveyances — and that happens 2 full business days after all funds have been received and verified by escrow.

Here's the timeline: You sign your loan documents. Your lender reviews the signed docs (1–2 days). The lender wires the loan proceeds to escrow. Escrow verifies that all funds — mortgage proceeds plus your closing costs cash — have been received as "good funds." Then there's a mandatory 2-business-day waiting period before the transaction can record at the Bureau of Conveyances. Once it records, you officially own the home. Then — and only then — do you get your keys.

This means "closing day" in Hawaii is typically 3–5 business days after you sign your loan documents. If you sign on a Monday, you might not get your keys until Thursday or Friday. If you sign on a Wednesday, you might not get keys until the following Monday or Tuesday because weekends don't count.

**By the Book:** Per VA Pamphlet 26-7, Chapter 9 (Legal Instruments, Liens, Escrows, and Related Issues), escrow-based closings are the standard in Hawaii. The delayed recording timeline is a function of Hawaii state law and the Bureau of Conveyances process — not a VA requirement. It applies to all real estate transactions in Hawaii, regardless of loan type. Most Hawaii residential properties record at the Bureau of Conveyances. Some older properties with Torrens title record at Land Court. Your escrow officer handles this distinction.

## Why This Matters for Your Planning

The delayed recording timeline affects everything: your rate lock period needs to be long enough to cover it, your lease expiration or temporary housing needs to account for it, and your moving timeline should build in a buffer. If you're PCS'ing and your TLA runs out the day you "sign closing documents," you may still not have keys for several days.

Work with a lender and agent who know Hawaii. An experienced team will set proper expectations from day one and align your rate lock, housing timeline, and escrow schedule.

## Getting Your Funds to Escrow

One more Hawaii-specific detail that catches mainland buyers off guard: if you're paying your closing costs with a cashier's check, it must be drawn on a local Hawaii bank. Escrow companies in Hawaii do not accept out-of-state cashier's checks. If your savings are at USAA or a mainland bank, you have two options: wire the funds directly to escrow, or transfer the money to a local Hawaii bank account and get a cashier's check from there. Navy Federal has local branches on Oahu, so this option is acceptable for a cashier's check.

Wire transfer is the preferred method. It's faster and avoids check hold issues. But this comes with an important warning: be vigilant about wire fraud. FBI IC3 data shows real estate wire fraud is among the fastest-growing forms of cybercrime, with hundreds of millions of dollars stolen annually from homebuyers who sent their closing funds to fraudulent accounts.

Here's how it works: a scammer compromises your real estate agent's, lender's, or escrow officer's email account and sends you "updated wire instructions" that route your closing funds to the scammer's account. The email looks legitimate — correct logos, correct names, correct transaction details. By the time anyone realizes the money went to the wrong place, it's gone.

The rule is simple: treat ANY emailed wire instructions as a potential phishing attempt until you've verified them by phone. Call your escrow officer directly at a number you've independently confirmed — not a number from the email itself. Verify the routing number, account number, and bank name before you send a single dollar. Your escrow company will understand this precaution and welcome the verification call.

## PROPERTY TAXES IN HAWAII

### Hawaii's Tax Advantage

Here's some genuinely good financial news: Hawaii has some of the lowest property tax rates in the nation, and Oahu is the lowest-taxed island — where most military members live and buy.

Oahu's nominal residential property tax rate is $3.50 per $1,000 of assessed value (0.35%). But once you apply the homeowner exemption — which reduces your assessed value by $120,000 — the effective rate on a typical purchase is even lower. On a $600,000 home, the exemption brings your taxable assessed value to $480,000, yielding approximately $1,680 per year in property taxes. Compare that to Texas at roughly 1.8% (approximately $10,800 on a $600,000 home), or New Jersey at over 2.4%, and you can see what a significant advantage this is. Hawaii's low property taxes are one of the hidden benefits of homeownership here that most mainland buyers don't discover until they run the numbers.

### The Homeowner Exemption — File This Immediately

File for the homeowner exemption with the City and County of Honolulu Real Property Assessment Division immediately after closing — it's not automatic.

The exemption reduces your assessed value by $120,000 ($160,000 if age 65+, effective July 2025). But the tax savings isn't the most important part.

Here's why it matters: without it, properties over $1 million get reclassified to "Residential A" (the investment property rate) — significantly higher than standard residential. The exemption keeps your property in the lower category, saving thousands yearly.

The filing deadline on Oahu is September 30th, and the exemption takes effect July 1st of the following tax year. Don't wait — file as soon as you close on your home.

### 100% VA Disabled Veterans — An Incredible Benefit

With a 100% VA disability rating, Honolulu County reduces annual property taxes to just $300 per year — that's $25 a month. On a property that would otherwise generate several thousand dollars in annual taxes, this is an enormous benefit.

The filing deadline for the disabled veteran exemption is different from the standard homeowner exemption. You can file by June 30th for it to take effect July 1st, or by December 31st for it to take effect January 1st. Important: this exemption must be filed in person at a satellite City Hall location on Oahu. Bring your VA disability rating documentation, and the staff will walk you through the process.

Seniors age 65 and older may qualify for additional reductions beyond the standard homeowner exemption. If you or your spouse qualifies, check with the Real Property Assessment Division about the enhanced senior exemption — it can provide meaningful additional savings.

## UNDERSTANDING IMPOUNDS — PLAIN AND SIMPLE

If you've never owned a home, the concept of impounds (also called an "escrow account" — a different use of "escrow" than closing) can seem complicated. It's not.

When you get a mortgage, your lender sets up an impound account for your property taxes and homeowner's insurance. Instead of paying your property taxes and insurance in one or two big lump sums each year, your lender divides those annual costs by 12 and adds that portion to your monthly mortgage payment. Each month, that extra amount goes into a special holding account managed by your lender. When your property tax bill or insurance premium comes due, your lender pays it directly from that account on your behalf.

Think of it like a savings jar: you put a little in each month so the money's ready when the big bills arrive. You never have to worry about coming up with large lump sums, and you never risk missing a payment.

Your monthly statement shows PITI: principal, interest, taxes, and insurance — the number your lender used for your DTI calculation. For condos, add HOA fees on top.

The lender reviews your account annually and adjusts your payment if taxes or insurance rates change. Shortages result in small increases; surpluses yield small refunds. These adjustments are normal and modest.

Most VA loans require impound accounts. There's a good reason: they protect both you and the lender. Taxes and insurance stay paid, you avoid surprise large bills, and impounds eliminate the risk of missed payments that could result in tax liens or lapsed coverage.

> **Hawaii Insider:** "I've had clients push back on impounds because they want to manage their own money. I get it. But impounds make homeownership stress-free. Your taxes and insurance are always current, you never miss a deadline, and your payment is completely predictable. One thing to remember, the HOA dues are not impounded, you pay these separately to the homeowners association."

## BUDGETING FOR LIFE IN HAWAII — BEYOND THE MORTGAGE

Your mortgage payment is the biggest line item, but it's not the only one that's different in Hawaii. Smart budgeting means understanding the full picture before you close — not three months after when the credit card bills arrive.

### Utilities

Electricity in Hawaii is significantly more expensive than the mainland — roughly two to three times the national average, driven by the state's dependence on imported fuel. A typical three-bedroom home on Oahu can run $250–$400 per month in electricity depending on AC usage, and condos typically run lower due to smaller square footage and shared building systems. Water and sewer are more modest, usually $60–$100 per month for a single-family home. If the property has solar panels (owned, not leased), your electric bill drops dramatically — another reason solar ownership is an asset in Hawaii.

## Groceries and Everyday Costs

Nearly everything consumed in Hawaii is shipped in, which drives grocery prices 30–50% above mainland averages. A gallon of milk, a loaf of bread, a pound of chicken — all cost noticeably more. Gas prices typically run $1.00–$1.50 per gallon higher than the mainland average. Dining out is similarly elevated.

The offset: your BAH is calculated for Hawaii's cost of living. COLA (Cost of Living Allowance) further supplements your pay specifically because the Department of Defense recognizes Hawaii's higher expenses. Together, BAH and COLA are designed to bridge the gap — but only if you budget intentionally. Military families who track their spending from the first month consistently tell me they do better than those who "figure it out as they go."

## Insurance Costs

As covered in Chapter 9, insurance in Hawaii runs higher than most mainland markets. Budget $400–$750 per year for a standard HO-6 condo policy, and $1,500–$4,000+ for single-family home coverage depending on location, construction type, and whether you need separate flood policies. These costs are typically impounded into your monthly payment, so they're already factored into your PITI — but know what they are so your total housing cost doesn't surprise you.

## HOA Fees

If you're buying a condo, HOA fees are a significant monthly expense — typically \$400–\$900 per month for a standard Oahu high-rise, and sometimes more for buildings with extensive amenities, older infrastructure, or ongoing maintenance reserves. These fees cover building insurance, common area maintenance, water and sewer (often included), elevator maintenance, security, landscaping, and reserve contributions. HOA fees are not optional and they're not static — they increase over time as building costs rise. Factor the current HOA fee into your budget and assume modest annual increases.

## The "All-In" Monthly Number

When evaluating whether a property fits your budget, calculate the all-in monthly cost: mortgage principal and interest, property taxes, homeowner's insurance (or HO-6), HOA fees if applicable, plus estimated utilities. Then compare that total to your BAH plus any COLA and other income you're directing toward housing. The gap between your all-in housing cost and your total available income is what funds everything else — groceries, gas, childcare, savings, and actually enjoying life in Hawaii.

**From the Closing Table: The Budget That Made It Work**

An Army Staff Sergeant — E-6 with 10 years of service — came to me convinced he couldn't afford to buy on Oahu. His BAH was around \$3,300 per month, and every property he looked at seemed to push his total housing cost above that number. We sat down and ran the real numbers: a \$475,000 two-bedroom condo in Ewa Beach with a \$340 HOA fee. His mortgage payment including taxes and insurance came to roughly \$2,850, plus the HOA brought his all-in to about \$3,190. That left \$110 of his BAH untouched — tight, but his COLA added another \$800 per month that he hadn't factored in. Once he saw the complete picture — BAH plus COLA minus all-in housing — he had real breathing room. He closed 35 days later and has been in that condo for three years now, building equity every month instead of paying rent.

## THE BOTTOM LINE

The financial side of buying a home in Hawaii has a few more moving parts than the mainland — the escrow process is different, the recording timeline adds days to your closing, and the funding logistics require advance planning. But none of it is difficult once you understand how it works.

Plan for 1.5–2% of the purchase price in closing costs and prepaids. Understand that "closing day" in Hawaii means 3–5 business days after you sign, not the same day. Wire your funds to escrow rather than dealing with cashier's checks. File your homeowner exemption the moment you close. And let impounds handle the budgeting for your taxes and insurance so you can focus on enjoying your new home.

The biggest advantage you have in all of this is working with a lender and an agent who know Hawaii's system inside and out. When everyone on your team understands the timeline, the process, and the requirements, the financial logistics become routine — and you can focus on the exciting part: moving into your new home in paradise.

## ACTION ITEMS

1. **Budget for closing costs now.** Even with zero down, plan to have at least 1.5–2% of your expected purchase price in liquid savings for closing costs and prepaids. On a $600,000 purchase, that's $9,000–$12,000. If cash is tight, discuss seller concessions with your agent — remember, the seller can pay normal closing costs and discount points beyond the 4% concession cap.

2. **Prepare your earnest money deposits.** You'll need approximately $1,000 for the initial deposit when escrow opens, and $5,000 or more for the subsequent deposit after the inspection contingency (J-1) is signed off. Both deposits are credited toward your final cash to close — they're not additional costs.
3. **Set up a local Hawaii bank account or plan to wire funds.** If your savings are at a mainland bank, ensure over-the-phone wire transfers are available well before closing — or open a local Hawaii bank account and transfer funds in advance. Escrow companies in Hawaii do not accept out-of-state cashier's checks. Always verify wire instructions by phone to protect against wire fraud.
4. **Understand your closing cost breakdown before you sign.** Your lender is required to provide a Loan Estimate and a Closing Disclosure that itemize every charge. Review these documents carefully, ask questions about anything you don't understand, and confirm that all charges comply with VA guidelines. No surprises at the signing table.
5. **Build the delayed recording timeline into your plans.** After you sign loan documents, plan for 3–5 business days before you get keys. Coordinate your lease expiration, TLA, temporary housing, and moving timeline around this reality — not around the signing date.
6. **File your homeowner exemption immediately after closing.** The deadline on Oahu is September 30th, with the exemption taking effect July 1st of the following year. This keeps your property in the lower residential tax category and saves you thousands per year. The exemption reduces your assessed value by $120,000 ($160,000 if age 65+). If you have a 100% VA disability rating, file for the disabled veteran exemption in person at a satellite City Hall — your property taxes drop to just $300 per year.

# 11

# ASSEMBLING YOUR TEAM AND FINDING YOUR HOME

You can be the most financially prepared, VA-educated buyer on the island — and still have a miserable experience if you're working with the wrong people. Buying a home in Hawaii is a team sport, and the quality of your team determines whether the process feels like a well-executed mission or a slow-motion disaster.

## YOUR REAL ESTATE DREAM TEAM

### The Buyer's Agent — Your Boots on the Ground

Your buyer's agent is your guide, your negotiator, and your advocate. In Hawaii, finding an agent who knows military buyers and VA transactions isn't a nice-to-have — it's essential. The Hawaii market has complexities that mainland agents never encounter: leasehold vs. fee simple, CPR properties, VA condo approval requirements, HOA nuances, and a closing process that runs on a completely different timeline than the rest of the country.

A good Hawaii buyer's agent will know which neighborhoods work for your commute to base, which buildings have VA-approved condo projects, and which properties to steer you away from before you waste time falling in love with a leasehold unit or a condotel that isn't VA-eligible. They'll also know how to write offers that compete — and how to address seller concerns about VA loans before those concerns become deal-killers.

Ask potential agents whether they regularly work with VA buyers and whether they're familiar with the nuances of VA loans — things like VA appraisal requirements, VA condo project approval, and how to address seller concerns about VA financing. An agent who understands these details can advocate for you far more effectively than one who's learning on the fly.

## Your Lender — More Than Just a Rate

Full disclosure: I'm a Hawaii-based VA-specialist lender. Of course I'm going to tell you to work with one. But here's the thing — I'm also going to give you the tools to evaluate any lender, including me, to make sure they actually deliver what's promised. The questions below work whether you're sitting in my office or across the desk from any other loan officer in the state.

In Hawaii, your lender isn't just the person who gets you a good rate. A VA-specialist, Hawaii-based loan officer understands delayed funding, local escrow processes, Hawaii-specific property types, and the unique challenges military buyers face — from PCS timing to BAH qualification to condo approval submissions. Your lender and your agent need to communicate constantly, and that communication is much smoother when both sides understand the same playbook. A mainland lender who processes VA loans nationally might give a competitive rate, but without understanding Hawaii's recording timeline, your closing could get delayed or your rate lock could expire.

## The Supporting Cast

Your escrow officer manages the transaction from accepted offer to recording at the Bureau of Conveyances. In Hawaii, escrow companies are the neutral third party that coordinates everything — they're not representing you or the seller, they're working for the deal. A good escrow officer keeps all parties informed and on schedule.

Your home inspector evaluates the property's condition and identifies issues before you commit. In Hawaii, this means someone who understands tropical climate concerns — termites, moisture, salt air damage, mold, and older island construction quirks.

Your insurance agent helps you secure the right coverage for a single-family home (HO-3 policy) or condo (HO-6 policy). A local Hawaii insurance broker makes a real difference in coverage quality and pricing.

## How the Team Works Together

Communication between your lender, agent, and escrow officer is critical given the additional steps in a VA transaction — appraisal scheduling, condo approval verification, delayed recording, and the inspection-to-J-1 signoff sequence. When your team has worked together before and trusts each other's process, things move smoothly.

A VA-specialist lender can close a VA purchase in 30 days — the same timeline as a conventional loan. That's a real competitive advantage when making offers, since some sellers still assume VA loans take longer. Banks and credit unions typically cannot close VA loans under 45 days. When your lender can tell a listing agent, "We close VA loans in 30 days," it removes one of the biggest objections to VA offers.

Ask your lender to recommend agents they've successfully closed deals with, and vice versa.

## The 5-Question Vetting Checklist

Whether you're evaluating a lender or a real estate agent, these five questions will tell you quickly whether they know what they're doing in Hawaii's VA market:

**1. How many VA closings did you do in Hawaii last year?** You want someone who does this regularly, not someone who closed one VA loan two years ago and considers themselves experienced. Volume matters because it builds the pattern recognition that prevents mistakes.

**2. Have you submitted VA condo project approvals?** In Hawaii, where condos dominate the market, this is a critical capability. If your lender or agent has never navigated the condo approval process, you're at a disadvantage on a significant portion of available inventory.

**3. What's your average days-to-close on a VA loan in Hawaii?** If the answer is "60 days" or "it depends," keep looking. An experienced VA-specialist lender should be able to close in 30–35 days consistently. That speed is a competitive advantage when making offers.

**4. Do you know what J-1 means without me explaining it?** This is your Hawaii-specific litmus test. If they hesitate or need to look it up, they don't know Hawaii's purchase contract process well enough to guide you through it.

**5. Will you give me references from veteran clients who bought in Hawaii?** Anyone confident in their track record will say yes without hesitation. Call those references and ask how the process went — you'll learn more in a 5-minute phone call than in any marketing material.

## HOUSE HUNTING IN HAWAII

### Starting Your Search

The primary resource in Hawaii is the HiCentral MLS — the database that feeds listings to Zillow, Realtor.com, and local brokerage websites. These sites are good starting points, but listing descriptions won't always flag whether a property is leasehold, whether the condo project is VA-approved, or whether the HOA is financially healthy. That's where your agent and lender earn their keep.

If you're PCS'ing to Hawaii, start your search months before you arrive. Many buyers work with an agent remotely via video tours and FaceTime walkthroughs to get a head start, then hit the ground running when they arrive.

## Neighborhoods and Communities Near Military Installations

One of the first questions every military buyer asks is, "Where should I live?" The answer depends on where you're stationed, your budget, your family's needs, and how much time you're willing to spend in traffic. Here's a quick overview of the major areas:

**Ewa Beach and Kapolei** are on the west side of Oahu and offer some of the newest construction and most family-friendly neighborhoods on the island. Commute to Joint Base Pearl Harbor-Hickam is reasonable. Commute to Schofield Barracks is manageable. Prices are generally more accessible than Honolulu proper, and there's a strong military community in the area.

**Mililani and Wahiawa** are central Oahu, close to Schofield Barracks and Wheeler Army Airfield. Mililani is a planned community with good schools, parks, and a suburban feel. Wahiawa is more affordable and sits right outside the gate. If Schofield is your duty station, this area makes a lot of sense.

**Aiea, Pearl City, and Salt Lake/Moanalua** are all convenient to Pearl Harbor-Hickam, Tripler Army Medical Center, Fort Shafter, and Camp Smith. These are established neighborhoods with a mix of single-family homes and condos. Salt Lake in particular has a high concentration of military families due to its proximity to multiple installations.

**Kailua and Kaneohe** are on the windward (east) side, close to Marine Corps Base Hawaii (MCBH). Kailua is one of the most desirable neighborhoods on the island — beautiful beaches, charming town, great restaurants — and the prices reflect that. Kaneohe is more affordable and still offers easy access to MCBH.

### Island Geography — What the Listings Don't Tell You

Oahu is only about 44 miles long and 30 miles wide, but the H-1 freeway crawls during rush hour. A commute from Ewa Beach to Kailua could take well over an hour. Windward to leeward means dealing with the H3 or Pali Highway through the mountains.

The island also has dramatic micro-climates. Windward side (Kailua, Kaneohe) gets significantly more rain than the leeward side (Ewa Beach, Kapolei). This affects your daily experience, home maintenance, and insurance considerations.

### Making a Realistic Wish List

Hawaii requires more compromise than mainland markets. The $400,000 single-family home with a big yard near Fort Campbell doesn't exist here. Many military buyers end up in condos or townhomes and discover benefits like lower maintenance, resort-style amenities, and walkability.

Separate your wish list into "must-haves" (bedrooms, commute time, school district) and "nice-to-haves" (view, garage, yard). Your agent can help calibrate expectations based on your budget.

## MAKING AN OFFER IN A COMPETITIVE MARKET

### Hawaii's Market Reality

Oahu has finite land and steady demand driven by military PCS cycles, local buyers, investors, and mainland transplants. Inventory is limited and desirable properties move quickly. Multiple-offer situations are common near military installations. Buyers who understand the competitive dynamics and come in with a strong strategy have a significant advantage.

## What Makes a Strong Offer

A strong offer includes a solid pre-approval letter from a reputable, Hawaii-based lender (not a generic pre-qualification), flexibility on the escrow timeline, and reasonable contingencies. Your agent will help calibrate each element based on the specific property and situation.

## Addressing Seller Concerns About VA Loans

Some listing agents and sellers still have outdated perceptions about VA loans, worrying about stricter appraisals or longer timelines. Most of these concerns are based on how VA loans worked years ago, not today.

Your agent and lender can address these concerns with education. A well-prepared lender can explain the VA appraisal timeline and the reliability of VA-backed transactions. A strong pre-approval letter from a known local lender tells the seller that a VA specialist has already vetted this buyer and the deal will close.

> **By the Book:** Per VA Pamphlet 26-7, the VA appraisal process is designed to protect both the veteran and the lender by ensuring the property meets Minimum Property Requirements (MPRs) and is worth the purchase price. This isn't a barrier to the transaction — it's a safeguard. In practice, the vast majority of VA appraisals come back at or above the contract price, and the process runs on a similar timeline to conventional appraisals.

## The Purchase Contract — Key Terms to Understand

Key contingencies in a purchase contract include the inspection contingency (your right to have the home inspected and negotiate repairs — the J-1 process from Chapter 10), the appraisal contingency (your protection if the VA appraisal comes in below purchase price), the financing contingency (protection if the loan doesn't get approved), and the closing date.

Your agent will walk you through every line of the contract before you sign. Understanding what you're agreeing to is essential.

**Hawaii Insider:** "I tell my clients to think of the offer like an operations order. You need to understand the mission (what you're buying), the timeline (when everything needs to happen), the resources (your financing and cash to close), and the contingencies (your exit strategies if something goes wrong). Come in prepared, and the whole process feels manageable."

## THE BOTTOM LINE

The team you build and the preparation you bring will determine your experience as much as the home itself. Hawaii's real estate market rewards buyers who are prepared, decisive, and well-advised. A strong agent who knows VA transactions, an experienced VA lender who knows Hawaii's closing process, and a clear understanding of your priorities — that's the foundation for a successful purchase.

Interview agents, talk to lenders, ask questions. The right team protects you through the entire transaction and ensures you end up in the right home at the right price with the right terms.

## ACTION ITEMS

1. **Interview at least two or three buyer's agents before committing.** Ask whether they regularly work with VA buyers, whether they understand VA appraisal requirements and condo project approval, and how they handle competitive offers. Look for someone who communicates well and knows the Hawaii market inside and out.

2. **Start your online search early.** If you're PCS'ing to Hawaii, browse the HiCentral MLS months before arrival. Share listings with your agent for feedback on VA eligibility, leasehold status, and HOA health.
3. **Define your must-haves vs. nice-to-haves.** Separate non-negotiable requirements (bedrooms, commute, schools) from preferences (view, garage, yard). Flexibility on property type will expand your options significantly.
4. **Get your pre-approval locked in before making offers.** A property-specific pre-approval letter from a reputable Hawaii lender is one of the most powerful tools in your offer.
5. **Choose a lender who can close in 30 days.** A VA-specialist lender who can match conventional loan timelines gives you a significant competitive edge. When your lender can tell a listing agent "we close in 30 days," it neutralizes one of the biggest seller objections to VA offers.
6. **Prepare for competition.** Discuss offer strategy with your agent before you need it. Understand how escalation clauses work and how your lender can support your offer by communicating directly with listing agents about the strength of your VA financing.

# 12

# FROM ACCEPTED OFFER TO CLEAR TO CLOSE

Your offer was accepted. Congratulations — you're under contract. Now the real work begins.

This phase brings everything together: the inspection, the appraisal, underwriting, and a steady stream of documents between you, your lender, your agent, and escrow. Understanding what's happening behind the scenes reduces stress and keeps the timeline on track.

This chapter dives deeper into the three major milestones: the home inspection, the VA appraisal, and the underwriting process.

## HOME INSPECTION — HAWAII STYLE

### Why the Inspection Comes First

As we discussed in Chapter 10, your lender waits until after the home inspection is completed and the J-1 contingency is signed off before ordering the VA appraisal. This protects you from potentially being on the hook for the $900 appraisal fee if you discover something during the inspection that causes you to walk away from the deal.

That means the home inspection is the very first thing that

happens once escrow opens, and it sets the tone for everything that follows. Schedule it as soon as possible — on a 30-day closing, your inspector should be in the home within the first few days.

## What a Hawaii Home Inspection Covers

A standard home inspection covers the structure, roof, electrical, plumbing, HVAC, appliances, and general condition. But Hawaii requires special focus:

**Termites and drywood termites.** Hawaii's biggest inspection concern. The VA requires a separate termite inspection on all VA loans in Hawaii (typically seller-paid), and your general inspection should flag any visible termite damage or conditions conducive to infestation. Given year-round warm climate, drywood termites are significant — don't skip this.

**Moisture and mold.** Tropical humidity makes moisture intrusion common, especially on the windward side. Watch for water damage, condensation, poor ventilation, and mold in bathrooms, kitchens, and areas without good airflow.

**Salt air and trade wind damage.** Constant salt exposure degrades paint, metal fixtures, railings, and roofing. This is normal for Hawaii, but the extent matters — especially for older homes near the beach.

**Cesspools.** Rare on Oahu, but some Big Island rural properties still have cesspools being phased out under state law. Conversion to septic or sewer can be costly.

**Solar panel systems.** Is it owned or leased? Owned solar is an asset; leased solar creates a lien and complicates VA financing. The lease transfers to you and affects your DTI. Get your lender's review early.

## Negotiating Repairs

Major structural issues and safety concerns are non-starters for VA loans. A compromised roof, significant foundation problems, or active structural termite damage are usually deal killers unless corrected to the satisfaction of all parties.

Cosmetic issues and minor repairs are fair game for J-1 negotiation — either seller repairs before closing or seller credits for you to handle after move-in. Things like a leaking faucet, failing water heater, or worn flooring are commonly requested. Your agent will help determine what's reasonable.

Once both parties agree on inspection terms, you sign off on Paragraph J-1. The inspection contingency is satisfied, you make your subsequent earnest money deposit (typically $1,000 - $5,000 or more), and your lender orders the VA appraisal.

## THE VA APPRAISAL

### What It Is — And What It Isn't

The VA appraisal serves two purposes: a licensed, VA-approved appraiser determines the fair market value of the property and verifies that it meets VA Minimum Property Requirements (MPRs). This is not a home inspection. The appraisal is primarily for the lender's protection — it ensures the property is worth what you're paying and that it meets basic standards of safety and habitability.

Don't confuse the two. The home inspection is thorough and detailed — your inspector will look at everything from the water heater to the electrical wiring and plumbing systems. The appraisal is broader and more focused on value and basic condition. You need both.

> **By the Book:** Per VA Pamphlet 26-7, Chapters 10–12 (Appraisal Process, Appraisal Report, and Minimum Property Requirements), the VA appraisal is a critical component of the loan process. The appraiser's determination of value establishes the maximum amount the VA will guarantee for the loan, and the MPR review ensures the property provides adequate security for the loan.

## Minimum Property Requirements (MPRs)

Per Chapter 12 of the VA Lenders Handbook, the property must be safe, sanitary, and structurally sound. Key requirements include a structurally sound foundation, roof free from leaks or damage, proper drainage, no lead-based paint hazards for pre-1978 homes, adequate water supply and sanitary facilities, and that the property be legally considered real estate and "readily marketable."

In Hawaii, the termite inspection report (TIR) is separate from the VA appraisal — two completely different reports. The appraiser does not comment on termite inspections. What matters is whether the inspector found evidence of live infestation and whether treatment is recommended. Treatment comes in two forms: spot treatment for small areas (usually condos) or full tenting (usually single-family homes). Any recommended treatment must be completed prior to VA loan funding and is typically seller-paid.

Most Hawaii properties in reasonable condition pass MPR review without issues. The most common problems are deferred maintenance — drainage issues, minor safety concerns, or habitability items. If flagged, the appraiser requires correction before closing. Major MPR issues like a cracked window, peeling paint on pre-1978 homes, or a damaged roof aren't optional — they're VA requirements.

## What Happens If the Appraisal Comes in Low — The Tidewater Initiative

If the VA appraiser believes the property value may fall below the contract price, the VA has a built-in safeguard: the Tidewater Initiative.

Per VA Circular 26-17-18, when a preliminary assessment indicates value may come in below purchase price, your lender has 2 business days to provide additional comparable sales, market data, or other information supporting the purchase price. This proactive step prevents unnecessary low appraisals caused by incomplete data.

Having a strong lender and agent team matters here. An experienced VA lender and knowledgeable buyer's agent work together to respond quickly — pulling recent comps the appraiser may have missed, documenting improvements, and making the case for contract price. Your agent's local market knowledge combined with your lender's appraisal expertise gives you the best shot at supporting value.

If the appraisal still comes in low after Tidewater, there's a second option: the formal Reconsideration of Value (ROV) process. Your lender submits additional evidence to VA staff for review, typically 5–7 business days. Between Tidewater and ROV, you have two opportunities to support the value.

If the appraisal ultimately comes in below purchase price, you can negotiate a price reduction with the seller, pay the difference out of pocket, or walk away with your earnest money protected by the appraisal contingency.

**From the Closing Table: The Tidewater Save**

A Marine Gunnery Sergeant was under contract on a three-bedroom townhome in Kaneohe — $735,000 purchase price, solid comps in the neighborhood. The appraiser triggered Tidewater, indicating the value might come in low. We had 2 business days. His agent pulled three recent sales within a half-mile that the appraiser hadn't used. I packaged the comps with a detailed market analysis showing the upward trend in the area and submitted everything to the appraiser. The final appraisal came back at $740,000 — $5,000 above contract price. Without the Tidewater response, the appraisal would have come in low and the Gunny would have had to make up the difference in cash or hope the seller was willing to renegotiate. This is why your lender-agent team matters. Two business days, the right comps, and a deal that closed on time.

## Appraisal Timelines in Hawaii

Plan for 10–14 days in Hawaii. The pool of VA-approved appraisers in Hawaii is smaller than on the mainland, and scheduling can be tight — especially during high-volume PCS seasons. The J-1 sign-off timing matters: your lender needs enough runway after ordering the appraisal to receive it back, address issues, and keep closing on track.

## THE UNDERWRITING PROCESS

### What Happens Behind the Scenes

Once your lender has the appraisal, termite report, and all documentation, the complete file goes to underwriting. The underwriter reviews the total loan picture and determines whether it meets VA guidelines and the lender's requirements.

Per VA Pamphlet 26-7, Chapter 4, underwriting considers credit history, income stability, assets, residual income (unique to VA — covered in Chapter 3), and compensating factors. The underwriter asks: Can this veteran reasonably make these payments? Is the property adequate security? Does everything check out?

### Common Conditions

It's rare for an underwriter to simply approve a loan with no conditions. More often, you'll receive a "conditional approval" — the loan is approved pending a few additional items. Common conditions include homeowners insurance, updated bank statements showing the funds deposited into escrow clearing the account, a letter of explanation for a credit inquiry or address discrepancy, or a statement of service for active duty personnel.

Don't panic when you get conditions — they're normal and usually straightforward. What matters is how quickly you respond. Your lender will send you the list of conditions, and the faster you provide what's needed, the faster the file moves to final approval. In a competitive market where timing matters, sitting on a condition request for three days instead of responding the same day can be the difference between closing on time and asking for an extension.

**Jay's Pro Tip:** "When we send you conditions, treat them like a tasking from your commanding officer — urgent, important, and time-sensitive. I tell my clients to drop what they're doing and get me those items within 24 hours if possible. The underwriter can't move forward until every condition is cleared, and every day of delay pushes your closing date. Keep your phone on and your email open during this phase."

## What Your Lender Just Said — A Quick Translation Guide

During the underwriting phase, your lender will use terminology that can feel like a foreign language. Here's what the most common phrases actually mean:

**"Your file is in underwriting."** Your complete loan package has been submitted to the underwriter for review. You're waiting. Don't call every day — but do stay accessible.

**"We have conditional loan approval."** The underwriter has approved your loan but needs a few more items before issuing final approval. This is normal — not a red flag. Get the requested items to your lender immediately.

**"The rate is locked."** Your interest rate is guaranteed for a specific period (typically 30–45 days). What's locked: the rate and points. What might still change: closing costs, prepaid amounts, and the exact monthly payment if property taxes or insurance estimates adjust.

**"We're waiting on the appraisal."** The VA-assigned appraiser hasn't completed their report yet. Hawaii's limited pool of VA-approved appraisers means this can take 10–14 days. Patience.

**"We received a Tidewater Notice"** The appraiser has signaled that the property value may come in below purchase price. Your lender has 2 business days to submit supporting comparable sales. This is your team's chance to fight for value — not a death sentence.

**"You're clear to close."** Everything is approved. Final documents are being prepared. You're almost there.

### Clear to Close — The Green Light

When the underwriter has reviewed everything, all conditions are satisfied, and the loan meets all VA and lender requirements, you'll receive "clear to close." The loan is fully approved and final documents can be prepared.

Your lender prepares the closing disclosure, documents are drawn and sent to escrow, and your lender and agent coordinate with the escrow officer to schedule signing. From clear to close to signing is typically just a few days.

### Final Loan Documents and Signing

You'll sign documents at the escrow office or with a mobile notary. Your lender, escrow officer, and/or mobile notary will walk you through each document. Many local Hawaii lenders attend signings, an advantage of working with a local VA specialist. Key documents include the promissory note, mortgage (deed of trust on the mainland), closing disclosure, deed, and VA-specific documents. It is our job to walk you through the documents at signing.

Bring valid government-issued photo ID and sign your name consistently — this matters for recording purposes.

After signing: the lender reviews your documents, wires proceeds to escrow, and the 2-business-day recording period begins. Plan 3–5 business days between signing and keys.

## WHAT CAN GO WRONG — AND HOW TO PREVENT IT

Over 25 years, I've seen nearly every possible complication between accepted offer and closing. Most are preventable. Here are the most common problems and how to avoid them:

**The appraisal comes in low.** This happens more often than buyers expect in Hawaii's competitive market, where bidding wars can push prices above recent comparable sales. Prevention: your agent should help you calibrate your offer based on realistic comps, not just what the seller is asking. If you're offering significantly above recent sales, be prepared for the possibility and discuss your Tidewater and ROV strategy with your lender before the appraisal.

**The condo project isn't VA-approved.** You fall in love with a unit, go under contract, and then discover the building isn't on the VA-approved list — and the HOA documents reveal issues that make approval unlikely. Prevention: check VA condo approval status before making an offer. If it's not approved, have your lender evaluate feasibility before you commit earnest money.

**Credit changes during the process.** A new credit inquiry appears. A late payment posts. An account balance jumps. The underwriter pulls a credit refresh before closing and your profile has changed. Prevention: follow the financial freeze rules from Chapter 3 religiously. No new credit, no late payments, no large purchases, no co-signing from pre-qualification through closing day.

**Missing or delayed documentation.** The underwriter needs an updated bank statement or a letter of explanation, and the buyer is on a field exercise or TDY and can't respond for a week. Prevention: give your lender everything up front. Tell them about any upcoming periods of limited availability. If you're deploying for a training exercise during the closing period, set up a power of attorney and make sure your lender knows how to reach you.

**Solar panel lease complications.** The property has leased solar panels, and the lease creates a lien that wasn't disclosed early. The lease payment affects DTI, the lien complicates title, and the timeline stalls. Prevention: ask about solar ownership status before you write an offer.

The common thread: preparation prevents most problems. Work with a team that knows what to look for, and front-load the due diligence so surprises are rare.

## THE BOTTOM LINE

This is the most process-intensive phase of buying a home. Multiple moving parts — inspection, J-1 sign-off, appraisal, underwriting, conditions — need to come together on a timeline that works for everyone.

Your job is straightforward: respond quickly when your lender or agent needs something, stay accessible, and trust the process. With the right team — a lender who knows VA loans in Hawaii, an agent who knows the market, and an escrow officer who keeps things on track — the heavy lifting happens around you.

The finish line is close.

## ACTION ITEMS

1. **Schedule your home inspection immediately after escrow opens.** On a 30-day closing, aim to have the inspection completed within the first few days. Ask your agent for inspector recommendations, and specifically look for inspectors experienced with Hawaii's tropical climate concerns — termites, moisture, salt air damage. Remember: major structural and safety issues are deal killers for VA loans, so the inspection is your chance to confirm the property is viable before the appraisal fee is incurred.
2. **Understand the termite inspection report (TIR).** The TIR is separate from both the home inspection and the VA appraisal. Look for two things: whether the inspector found evidence of live termite infestation, and whether treatment is recommended. If treatment is needed — whether spot treatment for condos or full tenting for single-family homes — it must be completed before VA loan funding and is typically paid by the seller.

3. **Understand the J-1 sign-off process.** After the inspection, you and the seller negotiate any repairs or seller credits. Cosmetic and minor repair requests are common and low-risk — the seller can simply say no, and you decide whether to proceed. Once both parties agree, you sign off on Paragraph J-1, make your subsequent earnest money deposit, and your lender orders the VA appraisal.
4. **Ask about solar panels before you fall in love with a property.** If a home has solar, find out immediately whether it's owned or leased. Leased solar creates a lien and can complicate VA financing. Get this information early so there are no surprises during underwriting.
5. **Respond to underwriting conditions within 24 hours.** When your lender sends you a list of conditions, treat it as urgent. Updated bank statements, letters of explanation, signed documents — whatever is needed, get it back as fast as possible. Every day you delay is a day added to your closing timeline.
6. **Know your options if the appraisal comes in low.** The Tidewater Initiative gives your lender and agent team a chance to support the purchase price before the appraisal is finalized. If it still comes in low, you can negotiate a price reduction with the seller, pay the difference out of pocket, or walk away with your earnest money protected by the appraisal contingency. Discuss these scenarios with your team before the appraisal comes back so you're prepared either way.

# 13

# CLOSING DAY AND BEYOND — WELCOME HOME

You've made it. The inspection is done, J-1 is signed off, the appraisal came back, underwriting gave you the green light, and you're clear to close. After weeks of paperwork, phone calls, and document requests, the finish line is finally in sight.

But remember — this is Hawaii. The finish line looks a little different here.

## CLOSING DAY IN HAWAII

Your lender and agent coordinate your signing appointment at the escrow office. Closing funds must be wired or delivered via a cashier's check drawn on a local Hawaii bank — no personal checks or out-of-state cashier's checks accepted. Always verify wire instructions by phone to protect against wire fraud.

After signing, expect a 3–5 business day wait before the transaction records at the Bureau of Conveyances. Use that time productively: arrange utilities — Hawaiian Electric (HECO) for electricity and Spectrum, Hawaiian Telcom, or SpaceX for internet — in the days leading up to recording so they can go live on recording day. If you're in a condo, check whether any utilities are included in your

HOA fees. When the escrow officer calls to confirm recording, it's official: you are a Hawaii homeowner.

## YOUR FIRST 30 DAYS AS A HAWAII HOMEOWNER

If you're in an HOA community, read the house rules carefully. Move-in requirements can include specific elevator reservation times, loading dock access, and parking rules. Renovation restrictions vary by building and can be strict. Your property manager will provide a welcome packet — read it before making assumptions about what's allowed.

### Meeting Your Neighbors — The Aloha Way

Hawaii has a culture of community that goes deeper than most mainland places. Introduce yourself to your neighbors when you move in — and bringing food is a local tradition. A plate of cookies, malasadas from Leonard's, or a simple welcome gift goes a long way toward building relationships that make island living special.

Your neighbors will watch your place when you deploy, accept packages, and give you the real scoop on the neighborhood that no listing ever mentions.

### Home Maintenance — The Hawaii Rhythm

Owning a home in Hawaii comes with its own maintenance rhythm, shaped by the tropical climate. It's different from the mainland — not harder, just different. Think of it as the island version of winterizing pipes or shoveling snow, except the climate is working for you most of the time.

Near the coast, salt air accelerates wear on exterior fixtures and metal surfaces. When replacing fixtures, choose stainless steel or rust-resistant materials and you'll stay ahead of it. Gutter cleaning before rainy season (November–March) prevents water damage — a quick Saturday morning task or an affordable annual service call. Annual termite inspections are standard practice in Hawaii and well worth the modest cost, even after your initial purchase inspection. AC maintenance matters in Hawaii's humidity — regular filter changes and annual servicing keep your system running efficiently and extend its life significantly.

In a condo, the HOA handles exterior maintenance, common areas, and major building systems. Your responsibility is the interior — appliances, fixtures, and any upgrades you've made. That's one of the reasons condos are popular with military buyers: less maintenance means more time enjoying the islands.

### File Your Homeowner Exemption — Immediately

File for your homeowner's property tax exemption with the City and County of Honolulu Real Property Assessment Division as soon as you close. The filing deadline on Oahu is September 30th, and the exemption takes effect July 1st of the following year.

Without this exemption, properties over $1 million get reclassified into the higher-taxed "Residential A" category — which covers most Oahu real estate. Filing keeps you in the lower residential category and saves thousands per year.

If you have a 100% VA disability rating, file for the disabled veteran exemption in person at a satellite City Hall location — your property taxes drop to just $300 per year.

## THE LONG GAME: BUILDING WEALTH THROUGH HAWAII REAL ESTATE

### Making Extra Payments

Once settled, consider making extra principal payments when possible. Even one extra mortgage payment per year — applied directly to principal — shaves years off your payoff date and saves tens of thousands in interest. Even rounding up your monthly payment adds up over time.

## When Refinancing Makes Sense

Keep an eye on interest rates after you close. If rates drop meaningfully below your current rate, refinancing can lower your payment and save significant money. The VA IRRRL (Interest Rate Reduction Refinance Loan) is one of the simplest refinances available — minimal paperwork, no appraisal in most cases, and just a 0.50% funding fee.

> **By the Book:** Per 38 U.S.C. § 3709(c) and VA Pamphlet 26-7, Chapter 6, you cannot close on an IRRRL until two conditions are both met: at least 210 days have passed since the first payment due date of your original loan, AND you've made at least 6 consecutive monthly payments. Whichever happens later controls. In practice, this usually means about 7 months from your first payment. Even if rates drop right after closing, don't panic — track the market and be ready once you hit that threshold.

## The PCS Decision: Sell or Rent?

When you receive PCS orders to a new duty station, you'll face a critical choice: sell or keep the home as a rental?

If you've built equity and the market is strong, selling provides capital for your next home purchase. Hawaii's market has historically appreciated well over the long term.

If you have a low interest rate — when rates were historically low in 2020 and 2021 — keeping the home as a rental can be powerful. Low-rate mortgages combined with Hawaii's strong rental demand (driven by military PCS transfers) can generate positive cash flow and continued appreciation.

Tax considerations matter too. If you've lived in the home for at least 2 of the last 5 years, you may qualify for the capital gains exclusion — up to $250,000 for single filers or $500,000 for married filing jointly. Once you've been away more than 3 years, that exclusion closes and the property becomes a full investment property.

At that point, if you sell, consider a 1031 tax-deferred exchange. This allows you to roll proceeds from one investment property into another and defer capital gains taxes. The replacement property requires conventional financing (VA loans are for primary residences only), but it's a powerful strategy for building wealth without a tax hit. Consult a tax advisor — the rules are specific and time-sensitive.

## Building a Real Estate Portfolio with VA Benefits

Over a military career, use your VA benefit to build a real estate portfolio one PCS at a time.

The strategy is straightforward: buy home #1 with your VA loan. When you PCS, keep it as a rental. At your new duty station, use your remaining entitlement — or restore your entitlement — to buy home #2 with another VA loan. Repeat over 20 years, and you could own multiple properties generating rental income and building equity.

## Understanding Entitlement Restoration

This is one of the most-asked questions I get from service members planning their next PCS: "Can I keep my VA-financed rental and still use my VA loan again?"

The answer is yes — through either remaining entitlement or entitlement restoration. Here's how each works:

**Using remaining entitlement:** If your current VA loan uses only part of your total entitlement, you can use the remainder for a new VA purchase at your next duty station. County loan limits apply to the second loan, and your zero-down buying power depends on how much entitlement remains. This is the simplest path — no restoration needed.

**One-time entitlement restoration (38 U.S.C. § 3702(b)):** This is the powerful option most people don't know about. If you pay off your existing VA loan in full — typically by refinancing into a conventional loan — you can restore your entitlement even while keeping the property as a rental. This is a one-time benefit, meaning you can only use it once in your lifetime. After the one-time restoration, your entitlement is fully restored and you can use it for a new VA purchase at your next duty station with full zero-down buying power.

The most common approach: refinance your Hawaii VA loan into a conventional loan, which pays off the VA loan and frees up your entitlement. You keep the property as a rental investment, and you buy at your next duty station with a fresh VA loan. The conventional refinance will likely require equity in the property and may have a higher rate than your original VA loan, so run the numbers carefully.

**Standard restoration:** If you sell the property and pay off the VA loan, your entitlement is automatically restored. No limit on how many times you can do this.

Work with a lender who understands entitlement math. The difference between remaining entitlement, one-time restoration, and standard restoration can mean the difference between needing a down payment at your next duty station and walking in with zero down.

This strategy requires discipline, cash reserves, and careful property management. But the math is compelling. Zero-down purchases, no PMI, competitive rates, and multiple entitlement uses create advantages civilian investors don't have.

## VA Assumable Loans — A Long-Term Asset

**Jay's Pro Tip:** VA loans are assumable. If you lock in a low rate today and keep the home as a rental (after you have met the occupancy requirement by living in it for at least 12 months), that assumable loan becomes incredibly attractive if you sell later, especially if market rates rise. A buyer assuming your 4% loan when rates are 7% will pay a premium. It's built-in equity you didn't have to create through appreciation.

## ACTION ITEMS

1. **Verify your wire instructions by phone before sending closing funds.** Call your escrow officer directly at a number you've independently confirmed — not from an email. Wire fraud targeting real estate closings is real. Cashier's checks must be drawn on a local Hawaii bank (Navy FCU okay).
2. **Plan your move-in timeline around the recording date.** Expect 3–5 business days after signing before receiving keys. Coordinate lease end, temporary housing, and moving logistics accordingly.
3. **File your homeowner exemption immediately.** Visit the City and County of Honolulu Real Property Assessment Division website, enter your Parcel ID, and file before September 30th. If you have 100% VA disability, file in person for the $300/year rate.
4. **Read your HOA rules before moving in.** Know move-in procedures, parking, pets, and renovation restrictions. Reserve elevator and loading dock if required.
5. **Set up a home maintenance schedule for Hawaii's climate.** Budget for routine maintenance, schedule gutter cleaning before rainy season, arrange annual termite inspections, and service your AC regularly.
6. **Monitor rates but remember the IRRRL seasoning requirement.** You cannot close an IRRRL until at least 210 days after your first payment date AND you've made 6 consecutive payments (whichever is later). If rates drop early, be patient — the VA IRRRL is one of the simplest and most cost-effective refinances available.
7. **Think long-term about your VA benefit.** Before your next PCS, evaluate whether keeping the home as a rental makes financial sense. Capital gains exclusion closes after 3 years away. If held longer, consult a tax advisor about a

1031 exchange for conventional financing of another investment property. Talk to your lender about entitlement restoration if planning to buy again.

## A FINAL NOTE FROM JAY

Twenty-five years. That's how long I've been helping military families buy homes in Hawaii. It all started the same way: someone in uniform asking the question I hear more than any other — "Can I really make Hawaii home?"

The answer has always been yes.

I wrote this book because every service member and veteran deserves to understand the tools available to them. Your VA home loan benefit isn't just a perk — it's one of the most powerful wealth-building tools you'll ever access. In Hawaii, where the market can feel intimidating and the process has quirks that trip up experienced buyers, the right information makes all the difference.

This work is personal. I'm a veteran. My wife Michelle is a veteran. We know what it means to serve, sacrifice, and wonder whether the life you want is within reach. I can tell you: it is.

Whether you're a young E-5 just starting a family, an O-5 on your third PCS to the islands, or a retiree coming back to a place that felt like home — your VA benefit can get you there. Zero down. No PMI. Competitive rates. The same paradise everyone else pays a premium for.

Don't let your benefit go unused. Don't let anyone tell you VA loans are too complicated or Hawaii is too expensive. I've helped hundreds of military families prove that wrong, and I'd be honored to help you too.

Welcome to Hawaii. Welcome home.

Aloha!

— Jay Anthony Miller, CMA, MBA U.S. Army Veteran, OIF/OEF realitycents.com | www.jay-miller.com

# APPENDIX A

### VA LOAN DOCUMENT CHECKLIST

Have these documents ready before you start the pre-approval process. Your lender may request additional items depending on your specific situation, but this covers the essentials.

## ACTIVE DUTY SERVICE MEMBERS

- Statement of Service (from your personnel office)
- Most recent Leave and Earnings Statement (LES)
- W-2s (most recent 2 years)
- Federal tax returns (most recent 2 years) — only required if you have self-employment income, rental income, or other business related income used for qualifying
- Bank statements (most recent 2 months, all pages, all accounts)
- Valid government-issued photo ID (military ID or driver's license)
- PCS orders (if applicable)

## VETERANS

- DD-214 (Member Copy 4 — this is the version that shows character of discharge)
- W-2s (most recent 2 years)
- Federal tax returns (most recent 2 years) — required if self-employed or using rental income to qualify
- Most recent 30 days of pay stubs (from current employer)
- Bank statements (most recent 2 months, all pages, all accounts)
- Valid government-issued photo ID

## NATIONAL GUARD MEMBERS

- NGB-23 (Retirement Points Statement) or equivalent documentation showing 6 years of creditable service
- DD-214 (if activated under Title 10 federal orders)
- Statement of Service (if currently serving)
- W-2s (most recent 2 years)
- Federal tax returns (most recent 2 years) — required if self-employed or using rental income to qualify
- Most recent 30 days of pay stubs
- Bank statements (most recent 2 months, all pages, all accounts)
- Valid government-issued photo ID

## RESERVISTS

- Proof of 6 years creditable service or DD-214 showing Title 10 activation
- Statement of Service (if currently serving)
- W-2s (most recent 2 years)

- Federal tax returns (most recent 2 years) — required if self-employed or using rental income to qualify
- Most recent 30 days of pay stubs
- Bank statements (most recent 2 months, all pages, all accounts)
- Valid government-issued photo ID

## SELF-EMPLOYED / 1099 INCOME

- Federal tax returns — most recent 2 years (personal)
- Federal tax returns — most recent 2 years (business, if applicable)
- Year-to-date Profit & Loss statement (prepared by borrower or accountant)
- Business license (if applicable)
- 1099 forms (most recent 2 years)
- Bank statements (most recent 2 months, all pages, all accounts — personal and business)

Note: Self-employment income is averaged over 2 years using net income (gross minus business expenses). If your business is less than 2 years old, most lenders cannot use that income for qualification.

## ADDITIONAL DOCUMENTS (IF APPLICABLE)

- Certificate of Eligibility (COE) — your lender can usually pull this electronically
- Divorce decree and/or separation agreement
- Child support or alimony documentation
- VA disability rating letter (for funding fee exemption)
- Signed purchase agreement (once under contract)
- Reenlistment statement and commander's letter (if enlisted with less than 12 months until ETS)

# APPENDIX B

## HAWAII HOME BUYING COST WORKSHEET

Use this worksheet to estimate your total costs and monthly payment with 100% VA financing. Fill in the blanks with your specific numbers. Estimated Purchase Costs

Your Estimate Purchase Price

$________

VA Funding Fee (2.15% first use / 3.30% subsequent — enter $0 if exempt)

$________

Closing Costs (estimate 1–1.5% of purchase price)

$________

Prepaid Insurance (first year HO-3 homeowner's or HO-6)

$________

Prepaid Property Taxes (typically 6 months to seed impound account)

$________

Prepaid Interest (from funding date through end of month)

$________

Initial Earnest Money Deposit (typically $1,000)

$________

Subsequent Earnest Money Deposit (typically $1,000-$5,000)

$________**

Total Cash to Close (Closing costs+Prepaids - Earnest Money)

$________

Note: Earnest money deposits are credited toward your final cash to close — they're not additional costs. Also, the VA funding fee can be financed into the loan.

## MONTHLY PAYMENT ESTIMATOR (OR USE THE HAWAII SPECIFIC CALCULATOR AT REALITYCENTS.COM)

Monthly Payment Amount

Principal & Interest (realitycents.com/advanced-calculator)

$________

Property Taxes (annual tax ÷ 12)

$________

Homeowner's Insurance or HO-6 (annual premium ÷ 12)

$________

HOA Dues (if applicable)

$________**

Total Housing Monthly Housing Cost

$________

## BAH COMPARISON

Your BAH (with or without dependents)

Lookup at travel.dod.mil/Allowances/

$________

Your Total Monthly Housing Cost (above)

$________**

If this number is positive, your BAH covers your housing costs with room to spare. If negative, you'll need to cover the difference from other income (such as COLA).

# APPENDIX C

## KEY HAWAII REAL ESTATE TERMS GLOSSARY

**ADU (Accessory Dwelling Unit):** A secondary residential unit on a single-family property, such as a converted garage, basement apartment, or detached cottage.

**BAH (Basic Allowance for Housing):** A military pay allowance to offset housing costs, calculated by pay grade, dependency status, and duty station location. Hawaii BAH rates are among the highest in the nation.

**Bureau of Conveyances:** The State of Hawaii office where real estate transactions are officially recorded. All property transfers must record here (or at Land Court for Torrens title properties) to become legally effective.

**COE (Certificate of Eligibility):** The VA document that confirms a service member or veteran is eligible for a VA home loan and shows their available entitlement. Your lender can usually pull this electronically.

**COLA (Cost of Living Allowance):** A military pay allowance for service members stationed in high-cost areas. Hawaii COLA covers non-housing expenses and is separate from BAH.

**Condotel:** A condo unit in a hotel-operated building that functions as a short-term rental. Condotels are generally not eligible for VA financing.

**Conveyance Tax:** A State of Hawaii tax paid when real property is transferred. The tax rate varies based on the property value.

**CPR (Condominium Property Regime):** A form of property ownership governed by Hawaii Revised Statutes Chapter 514B. CPR properties have individual TMK numbers and deeds but share common elements with other units. All condos are CPR properties, and some townhomes and even single-family homes in planned communities are organized as CPRs.

**DTI (Debt-to-Income Ratio):** Your total monthly debt payments divided by your gross monthly income, expressed as a percentage. VA loans use back-end DTI only (all debts, not just housing). Typical approval range in Hawaii is 45–50%, with 60%+ possible with strong compensating factors.

**Entitlement:** The dollar amount the VA will guarantee on your behalf. Full entitlement means no loan limit; partial or remaining entitlement applies when you have a VA loan outstanding.

**Escrow:** Has two meanings in Hawaii real estate: (1) the neutral third-party company that manages the closing process, and (2) the impound account your lender sets up to collect monthly property tax and insurance payments.

**Fee Simple:** Full ownership of both the land and the building. This is the standard and preferred form of property ownership in Hawaii.

**Funding Fee:** A one-time fee charged on VA loans that goes directly to the VA to sustain the loan program. Rates vary by loan type and usage. Veterans with a 10%+ VA disability rating and Purple Heart recipients are exempt.

**HO-6:** A condo owner's personal insurance policy that covers the interior of the unit, personal property, liability, and additional living expenses. Required for virtually all condo purchases regardless of unit condition.

**HO-3:** A single-family homeowner's hazard and hurricane insurance policy that covers the replacement value of the entire dwelling, personal property, liability, and additional living expenses. Required for all single-family home purchases.

**HOA (Homeowners Association):** The governing body of a condo or planned community that manages common areas, enforces rules, and collects monthly dues from owners.

**IRRRL (Interest Rate Reduction Refinance Loan):** A VA streamline refinance that allows you to lower your interest rate with minimal paperwork, no appraisal in most cases, and a 0.50% funding fee. Cannot close until at least 210 days after the first payment due date AND 6 consecutive monthly payments have been made (whichever is later).

**J-1 (Paragraph J-1):** The section of the Hawaii purchase agreement that addresses the home inspection contingency. Signing off on J-1 means both parties have agreed on inspection-related terms and the buyer is proceeding with the purchase.

**Land Court:** An alternative recording system in Hawaii for properties with Torrens title. Your escrow officer determines whether your property records at the Bureau of Conveyances or Land Court.

**Lease Rent:** The periodic payment a leasehold property owner makes to the landowner for use of the land. Lease rent can increase dramatically at renegotiation, making leasehold properties risky.

**Leasehold:** A form of property ownership where you own the building but lease the land from a landowner. Common historically in Hawaii due to large estate landholdings. Generally should be avoided for most buyers.

**LES (Leave and Earnings Statement):** The military pay stub that details a service member's pay, allowances, deductions, and leave balances.

**Master Policy:** The insurance policy carried by a condo building's HOA that covers common areas and the building structure. Most Hawaii condos carry walls-in coverage (99.9% of buildings).

**MPR (Minimum Property Requirements):** VA standards that a property must meet to be eligible for VA financing. The property must be safe, sanitary, and structurally sound.

**Ohana Unit:** A secondary dwelling on a residential property, rooted in the Hawaiian tradition of multigenerational family living. Similar to an ADU. Must be legally permitted for separate financing consideration.

**PITI (Principal, Interest, Taxes, Insurance):** The four components of a standard monthly mortgage payment. Add HOA dues if applicable.

**Residential A:** A Honolulu County property tax classification for non-owner-occupied residential properties assessed above $1 million. Properties without a homeowner exemption on file may be classified here at a significantly higher tax rate.

**Residual Income:** The amount of income remaining after all major expenses are paid. Unique to VA underwriting — the VA requires borrowers to meet minimum residual income thresholds based on family size and region (Hawaii is in the West region).

**ROV (Reconsideration of Value):** A formal process allowing the lender to challenge a VA appraisal by submitting additional comparable sales or market evidence for VA staff review.

**SCRA (Servicemembers Civil Relief Act):** Federal law providing protections to active-duty service members, including a 6% interest rate cap on pre-service debts, foreclosure protection, and credit protections.

**Special Assessment:** A one-time charge levied by an HOA on unit owners to cover major repairs or improvements not covered by the reserve fund.

**Tidewater Initiative:** A VA appraisal safeguard (per VA Circular 26-17-18) that gives the lender 2 business days to provide supporting market data when the appraiser believes the property value may come in below the contract price, before the appraisal is finalized.

**TIR (Termite Inspection Report):** A report from a licensed pest inspector documenting any evidence of live termite infestation and recommending treatment if needed. Required on all VA loans in Hawaii and typically paid by the seller.

**TMK (Tax Map Key):** Hawaii's unique property identification number used by the county for tax assessment and property records. Every property has a TMK number.

**Closing Disclosure (CD):** A five-page form your lender provides at least 3 business days before closing that details the final terms of your loan, monthly payment, and all closing costs. Compare it carefully to the Loan Estimate you received earlier — significant changes may require a new 3-day waiting period.

**Escrow (vs. Impound):** In Hawaii, "escrow" refers to both (1) the neutral third-party company managing your closing and (2) the impound account your lender uses to collect monthly property tax and insurance payments. Context determines the meaning — "we're in escrow" means your purchase is in process; "your escrow account" means the impound account holding your tax and insurance funds.

**Loan Estimate (LE):** A standardized three-page form your lender provides within 3 business days of receiving your loan application. It details estimated interest rate, monthly payment, closing costs, and other loan terms. Use it to compare offers from multiple lenders — the format is identical across all lenders by federal requirement.

**Title Insurance:** Insurance that protects the lender (lender's policy, required) and optionally the buyer (owner's policy, recommended) against defects in the property's title — unknown liens, ownership disputes, recording errors, or other claims that could challenge your ownership. In Hawaii, title insurance is a standard closing cost.

**1031 Exchange:** A tax-deferred exchange under IRS Section 1031 that allows you to sell an investment property and reinvest the proceeds in another investment property without paying capital gains taxes at the time of sale. Replacement property must be financed with a conventional loan (not VA).

# APPENDIX D

## HELPFUL RESOURCES

## VA RESOURCES

- **VA Home Loan Eligibility:** va.gov/housing-assistance/home-loans/eligibility/
- **VA Condo Approval Search:** lgy.va.gov/lgyhub/condo-report
- **VA Pamphlet 26-7 (Lenders Handbook):** benefits.va.-gov/warms/pam26_7.asp
- **VA Funding Fee & Closing Costs:** va.gov/housing-assistance/home-loans/funding-fee-and-closing-costs/
- **Certificate of Eligibility:** va.gov/housing-assistance/home-loans/request-coe-form-26-1880/introduction
- **VA Regional Loan Center (Honolulu):** va.gov/honolulu-va-regional-benefit-office-at-spark-m-matsunaga-department-of-veterans-affairs-medical-center/

## HAWAII RESOURCES

- **Hawaii Bureau of Conveyances:** dlnr.hawaii.gov/boc/
- **City & County of Honolulu Real Property Assessment Division** (for homeowner exemption filing): realproperty.honolulu.gov
- **Hawaii Real Estate Commission:** cca.hawaii.gov/reb/

## MILITARY RESOURCES

- **BAH Calculator:** travel.dod.mil/Allowances/
- **COLA Calculator:** travel.dod.mil/Allowances/
- **Installation Housing Offices:** Joint Base Pearl Harbor-Hickam, Schofield Barracks, Marine Corps Base Hawaii (Kaneohe), Fort Shafter
- **Military OneSource:** militaryonesource.mil (housing resources, financial counseling, relocation planning)
- **Military OneSource Financial Resources:** militaryonesource.mil/financial (financial planning tools, tax preparation assistance)

## TOOLS & CALCULATORS

- **RealityCents.com** — Custom Hawaii mortgage calculators including custom Military Buying Power calculator, affordability calculator, rent vs. buy comparison, and advanced mortgage comparison tools. Plus a full knowledge base of Hawaii lending articles.
- **Jay Miller:** realitycents.com | www.jay-miller.com

# APPENDIX E

## VA PAMPHLET 26-7 QUICK REFERENCE — HANDBOOK CHAPTERS

For readers who want to verify any claim in this book or do their own deeper research, here are the 16 chapters of the VA Lenders Handbook (VA Pamphlet 26-7):

**Chapter 1:** Lender Approval Guidelines — How lenders get authorized to originate VA loans

**Chapter 2:** Veteran's Eligibility and Entitlement — Who qualifies and how much entitlement you have

**Chapter 3:** The VA Loan Guaranty — How the VA's 25% guaranty enables zero-down financing

**Chapter 4:** Credit Underwriting — DTI, residual income, credit standards, and compensating factors

**Chapter 5:** How to Process VA Loans and Submit Them to VA — Lender processing procedures

**Chapter 6:** Refinancing Loans — IRRRL, cash-out refinance, and seasoning requirements

**Chapter 7:** Loans Requiring Special Underwriting — Multi-family, joint loans, and special circumstances

**Chapter 8:** Borrower Fees and Charges and the VA Funding Fee — What you can and can't be charged

**Chapter 9:** Legal Instruments, Liens, Escrows, and Related Issues — Closing procedures and state-specific rules

**Chapter 10:** Appraisal Process — How VA appraisals are ordered and conducted

**Chapter 11:** Appraisal Report — What the appraiser evaluates and reports

**Chapter 12:** Minimum Property Requirements — Safety, structural, and habitability standards

**Chapter 13:** Notices of Value — How the VA communicates appraisal results

**Chapter 14:** Construction Inspection — Requirements for new construction VA loans

**Chapter 15:** Lender Appraisal Processing Program — How lenders manage the appraisal process

**Chapter 16:** Common Interest Communities, Condominiums and Planned Unit Developments — Condo project approval requirements

# ABOUT THE AUTHOR

**Jay Anthony Miller** — Certified Mortgage Advisor (CMA), MBA

Jay Miller is a U.S. Army veteran and one of Hawaii's most experienced VA lending specialists. As a Signal Officer, he served as Company Commander with the 516th Signal Brigade at Fort Shafter, Hawaii, and deployed to Kabul, Afghanistan as Deputy Director of Communications Commercialization for the 335th Signal Command and Camp Arifjan, Kuwait as S4 for the 160th Signal Brigade (OIF/OEF, 2007–2009).

Jay holds a BA in History from the University of Washington, an MBA from Embry-Riddle Aeronautical University, and earned his Certified Mortgage Advisor (CMA) designation. NMLS# 657301.

Over a 25+ year mortgage career in Hawaii, Jay has served at Mortgage Masters Hawaii, Wells Fargo Home Mortgage of Hawaii (Leaders Club member, Top 3 producer), Compass Home Loans (President's Club 2014–2021), Hawaii Mortgage Group (Top producer 2024–2025), and currently serves as Sales Manager at CMG Home Loans.

His career numbers speak for themselves: over 1,500 families served, more than $700 million in loans funded, a 4.9 client rating, and a 99%+ customer satisfaction rating.

Beyond lending, Jay has been an active community leader as a member of the Locations Foundation Advisory Board (2014–2025) and Executive Board member (2023–2025), coordinating volunteer efforts including Hawaii 3Rs public school beautification projects across the islands.

Jay and his wife Michelle — a fellow veteran — share a bond forged in service and a life built on adventure. When they're not working, you'll find them competing in full and half distance Ironman triathlons, golfing, boating, hiking, and soaking up island life.

Jay is known for being responsive, accessible, and proactive. His philosophy is simple: an informed homebuyer is a happy homebuyer.

**Connect with Jay:** realitycents.com | www.jay-miller.com


instagram.com/jaymiller_hawaii
facebook.com/realitycents
x.com/RealityCents
linkedin.com/in/jay-miller-534bb5173

www.ingramcontent.com/pod-product-compliance
Lightning Source LLC
La Vergne TN
LVHW100317210926
848480LV00003B/1165